my **revisi⏻n** notes

OCR AS/A-level History

ENGLAND 1547–1603
THE LATER TUDORS

Nicholas Fellows

⑤ HODDER
EDUCATION
AN HACHETTE UK COMPANY

Every effort has been made to trace all copyright holders, but if any have been inadvertently overlooked, the Publishers will be pleased to make the necessary arrangements at the first opportunity.

Although every effort has been made to ensure that website addresses are correct at time of going to press, Hodder Education cannot be held responsible for the content of any website mentioned in this book. It is sometimes possible to find a relocated web page by typing in the address of the home page for a website in the URL window of your browser.

Hachette UK's policy is to use papers that are natural, renewable and recyclable products and made from wood grown in sustainable forests. The logging and manufacturing processes are expected to conform to the environmental regulations of the country of origin.

Orders: please contact Bookpoint Ltd, 130 Milton Park, Abingdon, Oxon OX14 4SE. Telephone: +44 (0)1235 827720. Fax: +44 (0)1235 400401. Email education@bookpoint.co.uk Lines are open from 9 a.m. to 5 p.m., Monday to Saturday, with a 24-hour message answering service. You can also order through our website: www.hoddereducation.co.uk

ISBN: 978 1 5104 1640 6

© Nicholas Fellows 2018

First published in 2018 by
Hodder Education,
An Hachette UK Company
Carmelite House
50 Victoria Embankment
London EC4Y 0DZ

www.hoddereducation.co.uk

Impression number   10 9 8 7 6 5 4 3 2 1

Year   2022 2021 2020 2019 2018

Cover photo © Granger Historical Picture Archive/Alamy Stock Photo

Illustrations by Integra Software services

Typeset by Integra Software Services Pvt. Ltd., Pondicherry, India

Printed in Spain

A catalogue record for this title is available from the British Library.

My revision planner

Introduction

Unit 1: British Period Study and Enquiry

Unit 1 involves the study of a period of British history. At both A- and AS-level there are two sections to the examination. Section A is the Enquiry section and Section B is the Essay section. In the Enquiry section there will be four primary written sources and one question for the A-level examination and three primary written sources and two questions for the AS. Section B will consist of two essays of which you will have to answer one. The type of essay set for both AS- and A-level are similar, but the AS mark scheme does not have a Level 6 (see page 7).

The Later Tudors, 1547–1603

The specification lists the content of the Enquiry element, which is the Mid Tudor Crisis 1547–58, under three key topics:
- Key Topic 1 – The stability of the monarchy, 1547–58
- Key Topic 2 – Religious changes, 1547–58
- Key Topic 3 – Rebellion and unrest, 1547–58

The specification lists the content of the Period Study element, which is Elizabethan England 1558–1603, under four key topics:
- Key Topic 1 – Elizabeth and religion
- Key Topic 2 – The nature of the Elizabethan monarchy, government and parliament
- Key Topic 3 – Elizabeth's management of financial, economic and social affairs
- Key Topic 4 – Elizabethan later years, 1588–1603

Although each period of study is set out in chronological sections in the specification, an exam question may arise from one or more of these sections.

AS-level

The AS examination which you may be taking includes all the content.

You are required to answer the following:
- Section A: two questions. They are source-based questions and will require you to use your knowledge to explain, analyse and evaluate three primary sources. The first question will require you to consider the utility of one of the sources for a particular issue and is worth 10 marks. The second question will require you to explain, analyse and evaluate the three sources in relation to an issue and is worth 20 marks. The section is worth 30 marks.
- Section B: one essay question from a choice of two. The essays require you to explain, analyse and assess an issue, using your knowledge to reach a balanced judgement about the question. The question is worth 20 marks.

The exam lasts one and a half hours, and you are advised to spend slightly more time on Section A.

At AS, Unit 1 will be worth a total of 50 marks and 50 per cent of the AS examination.

A-level

The A-level examination at the end of the course includes all the content.

You are required to answer the ONE question from Section A and one essay from Section B from a choice of TWO questions.
- Section A is the Enquiry question and will contain four written primary sources. You will be asked to use the four sources to test a hypothesis by considering the provenance and content of the sources and applying your own knowledge to the sources to reach a judgement about the sources in relation to the issue in the question. This is the same as the AS Question 2 but uses four sources instead of three.
- The essay questions are similar in style and requirement to the AS essay question, except to reach the highest level you will need to show a more developed sense of judgement.

The exam lasts for one and a half hours. You should spend slightly longer on Section A than B.

At A-level Unit 1 will be worth a total of 50 marks and 25 per cent of A-level.

In both the AS- and A-level examinations you are being tested on:
● the ability to use relevant historical information
● the skill of analysing factors and reaching a judgement.

In the AS examination you are also being tested on your ability to analyse and evaluate the different ways in which aspects of the past have been interpreted.

How to use this book

This book has been designed to help you develop the knowledge and skills necessary to succeed in the examination. The book is divided into seven sections – one for each section of the AS- and A-level specifications. Each section is made up of a series of topics organised into double-page spreads.
● On the left-hand page you will find a summary of the key content you will need to learn.
● On the right-hand page you will find exam-focused activities.

Together these two strands of the book will provide you with the knowledge and skills essential for examination success. Words in bold in the key content are defined in the glossary (see pages 98–99).

▼ **Key historical content**

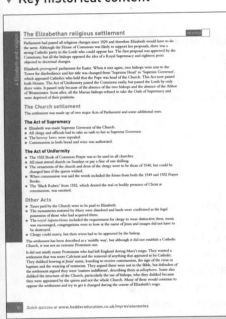

▼ **Exam-focused activities**

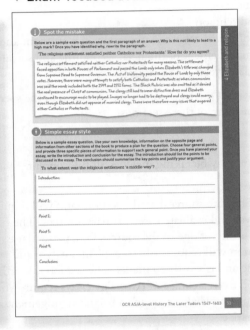

Examination activities

There are three levels of exam-focused activities:
● **Band 1** activities are designed to develop the foundation skills needed to pass the exam. These have a green heading and this symbol:
● **Band 2** activities are designed to build on the skills developed in Band 1 activities and to help you to achieve a C grade. These have an orange heading and this symbol:
● **Band 3** activities are designed to enable you to access the highest grades. These have a purple heading and this symbol:

Some of the activities have answers or suggested answers online. These can be found at www.hoddereducation.co.uk/myrevisionnotes. These have the following symbol to indicate this:

Each section ends with exam-style questions and sample answers with examiner's commentary. This will give you guidance on what is expected to achieve the top grade.

You can also keep track of your revision by ticking off each topic heading in the book, or by ticking the checklist on the contents page. Tick each box when you have:
● revised and understood a topic
● completed the activities.

Mark schemes

For some of the activities in the book it will be useful to refer to the mark schemes for this paper. Below are abbreviated forms.

AS-level

Level	Question 1 Utility	Question 2 All three sources	Question 3 or 4 Essay
5	Good focus, evaluation using provenance and context to engage with the issue to reach an analysis of its utility. **9–10**	Good focus, sources are evaluated using provenance and context, although there may be some imbalance, to reach an analysis of the issue. **17–20**	Mostly focused, supported answer with good analysis and evaluation to reach a supported judgement. **25–30**
4	Mostly focused, evaluated using provenance and context, with some imbalance to engage with the issue to reach an analysis of its utility. **7–8**	Mostly focused, sources are evaluated using some provenance and context to reach an analysis of the issue. **13–16**	Some focus with support, analysis with limited evaluation and judgement. **19–24**
3	Partial focus and evaluation of either context or provenance to produce a partial analysis of its utility. **5–6**	Partial focus and evaluation, some context to produce a partial analysis of the issue. **9–12**	Partial focus on the question, with some knowledge and analysis, but little or no judgement. **13–18**
2	Limited focus, general or stock evaluation to produce a limited analysis of the issue. **3–4**	Limited focus, evaluation is general as is context. General analysis of the issue. **5–8**	Focus is descriptive and may be more on the topic than the question. Any analysis may be implied. **7–12**
1	Answer is on the topic, basic evaluation and general knowledge. Simple or general analysis of the issue. **1–2**	Answer is on the topic, basic evaluation, much description of the sources and general contextual knowledge leading to a simple analysis of the issue. **1–4**	Focus on the topic and attempts at analysis will be little more than assertion. **1–6**

A-level

Level	Source question	Essay
6	Well focused, sources are fully evaluated using provenance and context to reach a fully supported analysis of the issue. **26–30**	Well focused, supported answer with very good analysis and developed evaluation to reach a supported and sustained judgement. **17–20**
5	Good focus, sources are evaluated using provenance and context, although there may be some imbalance, to reach an analysis of the issue. **21–25**	Mostly focused, supported answer with good analysis and evaluation to reach a supported judgement. **13–16**
4	Mostly focused, sources are evaluated using some provenance and context to reach an analysis of the issue. **16–20**	Some focus with support, analysis with limited evaluation and judgement. **10–12**
3	Partial focus and evaluation, some context to produce a partial analysis of the issue. **11–15**	Partial focus on the question, with some knowledge and analysis, but little or no judgement. **7–9**
2	Limited focus, evaluation is general as is context. General analysis of the issue. **6–10**	Focus is descriptive and may be more on the topic than the question. Any analysis may be implied. **4–6**
1	Answer is on the topic, basic evaluation, much description of the sources and general contextual knowledge leading to a simple analysis of the issue. **1–5**	Focus on the topic and attempts at analysis will be little more than assertion. **1–3**

1 The stability of the monarchy

The problem of Edward VI's age

In 1543 Henry VIII had issued a Third Succession Act which confirmed that if **Edward** died without heirs the throne would pass to Mary; 'and should the Lady Mary die without heirs, then the crown shall pass to the Lady Elizabeth and to her heirs'. This Act reversed the earlier Succession Acts, which excluded both **Mary** and **Elizabeth** from the succession, although it did not reverse their illegitimacy.

As Henry's health declined during 1546 he was aware that Edward would come to the throne as a minor. As a result, Henry wanted to try to avoid disputes about the succession and in his will confirmed the terms of the Third Succession Act.

The establishment of the Regency Council

Henry's concern about political stability was seen in his establishment of a **Regency Council**. This was balanced between 'reformists', led by Seymour (later **Duke of Somerset**), and the 'Catholics' under Norfolk and **Gardiner**. However, this was undermined by the actions of **Paget** and Denny, who left plenty of space in the king's will for changes to the king's wishes to be made and it appears that details about the Council were added only when the king was close to death and unable to prevent them. Moreover, their task was made easier as Gardiner had been removed and Norfolk was in the Tower.

The changes did not even require Henry's signature as Denny controlled the **dry stamp** of the king's signature, which could be inked in. He and Paget were also able to keep Henry's death quiet for a few days so the reformists were able to consolidate their position and Somerset establish himself and exercise virtual royal power.

The problem of a minor on the throne

There had been minors on the throne before:
- Henry III was nine when he came to the throne; civil war broke out but only after he came of age.
- Richard II was ten when he came to the throne in 1377; he was deposed in 1399 but that was because of his rule after he came of age.
- Henry VI was eight months old in 1422 and, although his reign witnessed the **Wars of the Roses**, England was relatively stable during the minority.
- Edward V was twelve when he succeeded Edward IV in 1483. He was imprisoned and probably murdered by his uncle and supposed protector, Richard III, which lost him support and aided Henry Tudor in his claim.

There were concerns a minor would create instability because:
- he would be unable to lead troops in battle
- other states might look to exploit the weakness of a minor and attack
- England might return to civil war as had happened in the fifteenth century
- a minor would not be able to control factional struggles, similar to those of the last years of Henry VIII
- in an age of personal monarchy, there were concerns about his image; it would be difficult to portray Edward as powerful or militarily adept.

However, the later image of him as a sickly child was not true when he came to the throne. There was every expectation in 1547 that he would reach adulthood and produce an heir.

The emergence of Somerset

Somerset's assumption of power was unsurprising as he was Edward's uncle and had built up a reputation as a successful soldier during the campaigns against Scotland in the 1540s. The transfer of power to him was smooth and there were good arguments against a Regency Council of sixteen with every member having an equal voice as it was very unlikely any decisions would be reached. However, some questioned the legality of his power as it went against Henry's wishes.

Mind map

Make a copy of the mind map below and use the information on the opposite page to show how each issue explains why there were concerns about a minor on the throne.

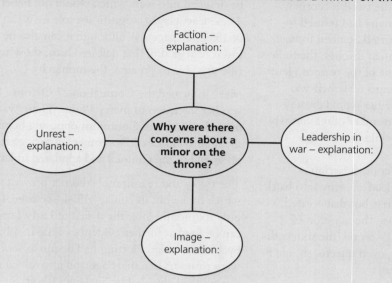

Faction – explanation:

Unrest – explanation:

Why were there concerns about a minor on the throne?

Leadership in war – explanation:

Image – explanation:

Spot the inference

High-level answers avoid just summarising or paraphrasing the sources, and instead make inferences from the sources. Below are a source and a series of statements. Read the source and decide which of the statements:

- make an inference from the source (I)
- paraphrase the source (P)
- summarise the source (S)
- cannot be justified from the source (X).

		I	P	S	X
1	Henry VIII's death caused unrest				
2	There were concerns among the Council on how to achieve stability				
3	The late king's will was enforced and Somerset became Lord Protector				
4	Edward was proclaimed king when his father's death was announced, the Council enforced the king's will and appointed Somerset as Protector				

SOURCE

From Edward VI's chronicle, 1547.

He [in his private diary Edward always referred to himself as 'he'] was suddenly proclaimed king on the day his father's death was announced in London, where there was great lamentation. He spent three weeks in the Tower while the Council enforced the late king's will. They thought best to choose the Duke of Somerset as Lord Protector of the Realm and Governor the king's person during his minority, being but nine years old. He sat at dinner with the crown on his head and Lords in the hall beneath.

The problem of gender and Mary's marriage

The accession of a female ruler did cause serious concerns in sixteenth-century society. England had been ruled by a female ruler only once before, in the twelfth century. That had resulted in civil war as many had refused to accept Matilda as queen and supported Stephen instead. Some countries also excluded women through the **Salic law** and it could be argued that one of the reasons Henry VIII was so concerned about having a male heir was because he believed that a female ruler would create dynastic weakness. There were a number of reasons why it was feared that a female ruler would weaken the monarchy:

- A woman would be unable to control faction.
- A woman would be unable to lead an army into battle.
- A woman was expected to marry, but that created further problems. First, there was the question of whom Mary should marry and, second, the sixteenth-century view was that women, even queens, should be subservient to their husbands.

This, therefore, raised two further problems:

- If Mary married an Englishman, the power of her husband's family would increase and they might dominate court.
- If Mary married a foreigner, there were fears that the country would be dominated by foreigners.

Mary's marriage

The Scottish theologian John Knox wrote *The First Blast and Trumpet Against the Monstrous Regiment of Women* in which he expressed his view that it was unnatural and insulting to God for a woman to rule. However, it was not that, but rather Mary's decision to marry Philip of Spain that caused the problems. There were only two realistic candidates:

- Edward Courtenay, Earl of Devon, who was backed by Gardiner.
- Philip of Spain, who was backed by Paget.

Courtenay was descended from royal blood, but Mary's preference was for Philip as the marriage would bring England closer to the Habsburgs, the family to which her mother, Catherine of Aragon, was related.

Philip might be a powerful ruler who could protect Mary, but as she was expected to be subservient she could be dragged into wars which would not benefit the nation. These fears played a significant role in Wyatt's rebellion of 1554 (see page 44), although it can also be argued that it was Mary's skill that defeated him, showing that female rule was able to preserve the monarchy.

Mary informed the Council on 27 October 1553 that it was her intention to marry Philip. There was a petition from the House of Commons opposing her decision, but she ignored it. On 7 December a marriage treaty was presented to the Council and approved in January 1554.

The treaty and reassurances did not prevent rebellion, which broke out in January 1554 (see page 44). This was only six months after the defeat of **Lady Jane Grey** and can be used as further evidence of the instability caused by a female ruler. Plotting had begun as soon as there were rumours of a marriage and it involved members of the political elite, led by Sir James Croft, Sir Peter Carew and Sir Thomas Wyatt. These men had all held office under Henry VIII and Edward, but now feared they would lose influence and be replaced by Spaniards who would dominate both court and government. The initial plan was a four-pronged rising based in Devon, Leicestershire, the Welsh borders and Kent, though it was only the latter that actually rose.

However, whether the proclamation of the marriage was the real cause is a matter of debate as Wyatt was a Protestant and the other leaders all had links with the reformed faith. The rebels had planned to marry Elizabeth to Courtenay, but he disclosed the scheme and this forced the rebels to act early. Despite this, the situation was serious as a royal force under Norfolk sent to confront the rebels deserted. The rebels did get to the gates of the city of London, but Mary's resolution and refusal to leave the city were factors in its defeat and again a sign that a female ruler was not necessarily weak.

Despite the defeat of the rebellion, it did have an impact on stability as the marriage did not take place until twelve months after Mary came to the throne and after the marriage Philip spent more time abroad than in the country, limiting his influence to, at best, a distant confidant.

Using the provenance

Sources A and B show different explanations given for Wyatt's rising. Identify the difference and use the provenance to think which might be more reliable.

Difference:

_____

_____

_____

Which might be more reliable:

_____

Why?

_____

_____

_____

SOURCE A

Thomas Wyatt explains the reasons for the rebellion, 25 January 1554.

We write to you as friends, neighbours and Englishmen, concerning Queen Mary's declared intention to marry a foreigner, and request you to join us to prevent this. We swear to you before God that we seek no harm to the queen, but merely wish her better advice. Our wealth and health depend on it. A hundred armed Spaniards have already arrived at Dover and travelled through Kent on their way to London. We require you to assemble with us as much support as possible, to help us protect liberty and the commonwealth.

SOURCE B

An account written for the government explains the rising. From John Proctor, A History of Wyatt's Rebellion, 1554.

Wyatt, proceeding in his detestable purpose, armed himself and as many as he could. And, considering that the restoring of the newly-forged religion was not a cause general enough to attract all sorts to support him, he determined to speak no word of religion but to make the colour of his commotion only to withstand strangers and to advance liberty.

AS question

Read Source C and answer the following question.

Source C refers to the defeat of Wyatt's rebellion. How useful is it for understanding why Mary Tudor was able to rally support against Wyatt?

SOURCE C

A contemporary records Mary's reaction to Wyatt's march on London. From Charles Wriothesley's Chronicle of England *for 1554.*

On 1 February the queen went to the Guildhall and declared to the audience the wicked plan of the traitor Wyatt, which was utterly to deprive her of her crown, and to ransack the city. She spoke so nobly, with so good spirit, and with so loud a voice, that all the people might hear her Majesty, and were comforted in their hearts with so sweet words which made them weep with joy to hear her Majesty speak. On 3 February the queen appointed Lord William Howard to be Captain General, with the Lord Mayor for the defence of the city.

The succession in 1553

In the early months of 1553 Edward VI's health began to deteriorate, and despite treatment, he continued to decline. According to the Succession Acts and Henry's will, the throne was to pass to Edward's half-sister, Mary. However, during the spring and summer a plot developed to change the succession so as to exclude Mary. Most accounts suggest that the scheme was the work of the Lord President of the Council, **Northumberland**. These accounts argue that he was behind it because:

- it was essential to preserve his power
- as a Protestant he would lose power when the Catholic Mary came to the throne.

These accounts have therefore argued that he arranged the marriage of his son, Guildford Dudley, to Lady Jane Grey in order to achieve it. This was soon followed by Edward changing his will and naming Jane Grey as his heir.

However, there is also evidence to suggest that Edward was the driving force behind the attempts:

- He was playing a greater role in government, attending Privy Council meetings and setting some agendas.
- Edward was a committed Protestant and wanted to stop the throne passing to his Catholic half-sister.
- Edward wanted the religious reform programme he had started to continue.

The Devise

The **Devise** for the succession was initially drawn up in May 1553. It named the male heirs of the Grey family as the successors, but there were no male heirs and there was no likelihood of any being born before Edward died, as his health was declining rapidly. Therefore, the initial Devise was altered and Jane Grey was made heir. It was only with this change that Northumberland's importance increased as, when Guildford married Jane, she was not heir.

The plot

The plot was poorly managed and this supports the view that it was Edward, rather than Northumberland, who was behind its organisation:

- As an experienced soldier, Northumberland would have ensured he had sufficient forces to take control, but the professional force had been dismissed in 1552.
- He would have ensured Mary was captured, but she escaped to East Anglia.
- He would have launched a propaganda campaign to prepare the nation for the change in the succession.

When Edward died on 6 July 1553 the news was kept quiet for two days. Mary responded quickly and proclaimed herself queen and sent letters to the Privy Council and important towns informing them, thus behaving as if she considered herself the rightful and legitimate monarch. The question of legitimacy was important for the ruling class, because if they supported an illegal claimant all laws could be challenged and their right to land questioned. It was in their interests to support the rightful ruler.

Although Jane was proclaimed queen, against her wishes, on 10 July, her rule did not last (see page 42). Mary also proclaimed herself queen and the rebellion soon collapsed.

Mary Tudor's death

If the death of Edward VI had created instability with the raising of armed forces, this was not the case in 1558. However, even in 1553 Lady Jane Grey ruled for only nine days and the ruling elite supported the rightful monarch, backing Mary once Northumberland left London.

In 1558 there was no attempt to alter the succession by Mary, although she did try to persuade Elizabeth to maintain the Catholic faith. When she died, the crown was offered peacefully to her sister, suggesting that legitimacy and the succession as stated by Henry in the Third Succession Act was more important than issues of religious belief.

! Support or challenge

Below is an exam-style question that asks you to agree with a specific statement and a series of sources relevant to the question. Use your own knowledge and the information on the opposite page to decide whether the sources support or challenge the statement in the question and explain why in the boxes.

Using these three sources in their historical context, assess how far they support the view that Mary's legitimacy was the most important reason people supported her in 1553.

Source	Support	Challenge
A		
B		
C		

SOURCE A

An anonymous writer explains why people supported Mary. John Foxe later used this as a source for his Acts and Monuments.

After King Edward's death the Council proclaimed Lady Jane as queen. But, partly because of the right of Mary's title and partly because of the malice that the people bore to the Duke of Northumberland for the death of the Duke of Somerset and his other cruelty, the majority of the commons with some nobles sided with Lady Mary, who proclaimed herself queen.

SOURCE B

A writer explains his concerns about the change to the succession. From A Poetical Autobiography of Sir Nicholas Throckmorton, *written before 1571.*

Immediately I heard of King Edward's death. I sorrowfully left Greenwich and went to our family home in London. My brother guessed by my depressed mood that the king was dead and I told them this was so. I revealed to them the cover-up that had taken place and how the Council intended to proclaim Queen Jane. I did not love Catholicism but detested the wicked plan to exclude rightful heirs. I was looking for a solution; there was no need to injure Mary in this way.

SOURCE C

A writer explains why Suffolk men supported Mary. From John Foxe, Acts and Monuments, *written in the mid 1550s.*

The first to resort to her were the Suffolk men who, being always forward in promoting the proceedings of the gospel, promised her their aid provided she would promise them no innovations would be made in religion. She agreed.

ⓘ Doing reliability well

Below are an exam-style question and a set of definitions listing common reasons why sources can be unreliable. Using Sources A–C above, for each source write a critical account of whether it is a reliable or unreliable piece of evidence, justifying your answer by referring to the definitions below.

Using these three sources in their historical context, assess how far they support the view that Mary's legitimacy was the most important reason people supported her in 1553.

- **Vested interest**: the source is written so that the writer can protect their own power or interests.
- **Second-hand report**: the writer is not in a position to know and is relying on someone else's information.
- **Expertise**: the source is written on a subject that the author is an expert in.
- **Political bias**: the source is written by a politician and it reflected their political views.
- **Reputation**: the source is written to protect the writer's reputation.

Faction and its impact during the rule of Somerset and Northumberland

The last years of Henry VIII's reign had seen a factional struggle, but this appeared to have ended with the triumph of Somerset and the 'reformist' faction over the 'Catholic' faction with the defeat of Henry's plan for a balanced Regency Council. However, although the reformists dominated government, the events of the summer of 1549 gave the Catholic faction an opportunity to reassert itself.

The impact of the 1549 unrest

Although the unrest in the countryside was put down, the ruling elite were concerned by the disorder, particularly as some of the rebels' complaints were against them. Not only that, but there was also disquiet within governing circles about the personal nature of Somerset's government, as letters from Paget, a close advisor of the Protector, reveal. It led to the formation of the anti-Somerset faction.

The anti-Somerset faction

The group that was formed had little in common, except a dislike of Somerset's methods and policies. It included such diverse figures as Paget, Warwick, who was made Duke of Northumberland in 1547, and Wriothesley. The latter was opposed to Somerset's religious policies, Warwick may have seen an opportunity to advance his own power, while Paget was concerned about Somerset ignoring his advice. It was the events of the summer of 1549 that provided this group with the opportunity to act.

Somerset's loss of power

As Somerset's hold on power declined, he retreated to Hampton Court with Edward. On 5 October he summoned loyal subjects there to defend him and the king, but moved the next day to Windsor with Edward. However, Edward fell ill, claimed he was a prisoner, and abandoned his uncle. Edward stated that Somerset had threatened riots if he was removed from power. Although Somerset denied this, he could not contradict the king and within a week was removed.

The triumph of Warwick

Although Somerset had been removed, Warwick's triumph was far from guaranteed. The Council contained a majority of religious conservatives who did not trust Warwick. He brought in his own allies so that he had a Protestant majority, but in early December there were rumours of a Catholic plot to remove him. Warwick seized the opportunity, declaring that any who attacked Somerset were attacking him. By January 1550 the leading Catholics, the Earls of Arundel and Southampton, had been dismissed and Warwick was Lord President of the Council. He placed his own supporters in important positions around Edward, but in order to succeed he had been forced to ally with more religiously radical members and this would impact on religious developments (see page 22).

Once he was secure he attempted a reconciliation with Somerset.

Despite the factional struggle lasting from October 1549 until early 1550, the administration of the country continued to function and did not impact on the efficiency of the government. The crisis in October was short-lived and did not threaten the monarchy.

The execution of Somerset

Warwick released Somerset from jail, his goods were restored and his daughter married Warwick's son. He was also restored to court and the Privy Council. However, Somerset continued to plot in an attempt to recover his position and this led the Privy Council to execute him on 22 January 1552, although some of the evidence may have been fabricated to justify his death.

Linking sources

Below are a question and the four sources referred to in the question. In one colour, draw links between the sources to show ways in which they show that political instability was caused by the ambition of councillors.

Read Sources A–D. How far do they show that ambition was the main cause of political instability in the period 1549–52?

SOURCE A

An advisor writes to Protector Somerset. From a letter from William Paget, July 1549.

The king's subjects out of all discipline and all obedience, and care for neither you or the king. What is the cause? Your softness, you wish to be good to the poor. It is a pity that your gentle approach should cause such evil as the rebels now threaten.

SOURCE B

A chronicle outlines the charges against Somerset in October 1549.

First that through his malicious and evil government, the Lord Protector had caused all the recent unrest in the country. Second, he was ambitious and sought his own glory. Third, that he had ignored the advice of his councillors. Fourth, that he had told untruths about the Council to the king.

SOURCE C

A contemporary relates the events leading to Somerset's execution. From a letter to John Calvin from Francis Bourgoyne, January 1553.

Somerset was the head of a conspiracy against the whole Council, and more particularly against the Duke of Northumberland, whom Somerset pursued with a deadly hatred, since Northumberland had been foremost among those who deprived him of the rank of Lord Protector.

SOURCE D

A contemporary explains why the Privy Council executed Somerset. From Francis Bourgoyne's further letter to John Calvin, January 1553.

The whole Council decided that they would no longer endure that excessive arrogance of the Duke of Somerset, that made it quite clear that if he were released from imprisonment, he would raise rebellions which would endanger the whole kingdom.

 Add your own knowledge

Annotate Sources A–D with your own knowledge to add evidence which either supports or challenges the view presented in each source about whether ambition was the main cause of instability in the period 1549–52.

Faction under Mary

One of the major concerns about a female ruler was that it was believed she would be unable to control factions. This had already appeared to be the case over Mary's proposed marriage with two of her leading councillors supporting different suitors. There were also fears that a Spanish marriage would create factional strife between English courtiers, worried about their positions and patronage and the expected influx of Spanish courtiers, who they believed would dominate the court and be given positions within the administration. Despite these concerns, there is no evidence that it had an impact on the efficiency of the administration.

Divisions within the Privy Council

Mary's Privy Council was large as she brought in her own supporters who had helped her gain the throne, but also kept many experienced administrators. This has led some to argue that it was ineffective. However, this view can be challenged because:

- it was rare for all councillors to be present
- the average size of meetings was similar to those held under Northumberland
- committees were established in 1554 which excluded casual councillors
- in 1555 an 'inner council' was established
- Philip's departure in 1555 and the death of Gardiner in November 1555 allowed Paget to dominate and establish a conciliar form of government.

Clashes between Gardiner and Paget

There were clashes between Gardiner and Paget, first over Mary's marriage, but also over the revival of the **heresy laws**. In April 1554 parliament rejected their reintroduction and did not agree to them until they had guarantees that monastic lands would not be restored to the Church. Many have argued that this provides clear evidence of the unpopularity of Mary's religious policies. However, the struggle to reintroduce them was part of the factional struggle between Paget and Gardiner, because the same legislation that had initially been rejected was passed once Paget and his supporters backed it.

However, despite the delay in introducing the legislation and the desire of Gardiner and Paget to persuade the queen to support their policies, they were able to put aside their differences for much of the reign.

The impact of Pole

It could be argued that the arrival of **Cardinal Pole** as **papal legate** changed the nature of court politics. It has been suggested that Mary was aware of the divisions among her councillors and therefore she had everything referred to him, or to the Spanish ambassador, Simon Renard, as she did not trust her councillors' advice.

However, debates over policy in the Privy Council were usually constructive and faction should not be viewed as a bad thing; after all her half-sister, Elizabeth, was able to use it to great effect to control government by playing one group off against the other. As with Edward's reign, there is no evidence to suggest that the struggles created inefficiency or prevented the government and administration from working.

Support or challenge

Below is an exam question which asks you a specific statement. Look at Sources A to D and decide whether the sources support or challenge the view. Fill in the boxes in the table below showing what statements in the source support or challenge the view. This is the first stage in answering the question and will not by itself gain high marks.

Using Sources A–D in their historical context, assess how far they support the view that Mary's government was weak and divided.

Source	Support	Challenge
A		
B		
C		
D		

SOURCE A

Mary rallies support against Wyatt, Guildhall speech, 1 February 1554.

At my coronation, when I was wedded to the realm, you promised to obey me. If a prince may as earnestly love her subjects as a mother loves her child, then be sure that I, your lady and mistress, love and favour you as tenderly. Thus loving you, I must think that you love me as faithfully; so I am sure we shall speedily overthrow these rebels.

SOURCE B

The imperial ambassador writes to the Emperor about English politics in 1554.

No attention is paid to the law; the queen and her Council are neither respected nor obeyed nor feared. The people say King Philip is not going to employ Englishmen, though he agreed to so in the marriage treaty. They proclaim that they are to be enslaved, for the queen is a Spanish woman at heart.

SOURCE C

The Venetian ambassador in a letter to the Senate, May 1557, gives an assessment of developments in England during Mary's reign.

Knowing of the divisions among her councillors, the queen, in order not to be deceived, ordered that Cardinal Pole should have everything referred to him, since she trusts him and distrust almost all others. The queen is greatly grieved by the conspiracies and plots formed against her daily. When she punishes the ringleaders, she provokes hatred since the offenders are excused by almost everyone.

SOURCE D

A modern historian assesses Mary's rule. From Glyn Redworth, 'Female Monarchy under Philip and Mary', English Historical Review, 1997.

At the beginning of her reign, Mary was a strong and decisive monarch. As her reign progressed, however, Mary's weakness became more apparent. Hit by illness and phantom pregnancies, the queen was seen as less able of imposing her will. The rivalry among her councillors is justifiably legendary. Meanwhile, Philip exercised effective control over his wife's choice of councillors.

 ## Add your own knowledge

Annotate Sources A–D with your own knowledge to add evidence that either supports or challenges the views presented in each source about whether Mary's government was weak and divided.

Exam focus (A-level)

Below is a model answer in response to an exam-style A-level question and sources. Read the answer and the comments around it.

Using Sources A–D in their historical context, assess how far they support the view that female rule was a serious problem in the 1550s.

SOURCE A

Edward VI issues his 'Devise for the Succession' setting out who shall succeed to the crown in the event of his death.

As Lady Mary and Lady Elizabeth are both illegitimate they have no claim to the crown. As half blood to us, they would be barred by ancient law and custom of this realm and could not succeed us even if legitimate. Were the said Mary or Elizabeth to have the crown of England and marry a foreigner, he would practise his own country's laws and customs within this realm. This would utterly subvert the commonwealth of this our realm. We therefore declare that the crown shall, for lack of issue of our body, come firstly to the eldest son of Lady Frances Grey or, secondly, to the Lady Jane Grey and her male heirs.

SOURCE B

Having disregarded her Council's advice to leave the capital for her own protection, Queen Mary addresses the citizens of London in her Guildhall speech, 1 February 1554, to rally their support against Wyatt's approaching rebels.

At my coronation, when I was wedded to this realm, you promised to obey me. If a prince may earnestly love her subjects as a mother loves her child, then be sure that I, your lady mistress, love and favour you as tenderly. Thus loving you, I must think that you love me as faithfully; so I am sure we shall speedily overthrow these rebels.

SOURCE C

The Act of Parliament for a marriage treaty between Mary I and Prince Philip of Spain sets out the terms to protect English interests.

This treaty greatly honours and benefits England. The prince shall enjoy, jointly, the style and honour of king. He shall happily help administer England, preserving its rights, laws, privileges and customs. The queen shall have total control of all offices, lands and revenues, and grant them to natural born Englishmen. Sincere friendship with Spain will be happily established forever, God willing, to benefit their successors. Should no children be born and the queen die before him, he shall accept the lawful heir. The prince shall take no jewels abroad, nor ships, guns or supplies. He shall renew defences of the realm. By this marriage, England shall not be entangled in war, and the prince shall observe England's peace with France.

SOURCE D

A Scottish Calvinist preacher expresses his opinion on female rule. From John Knox, The First Blast and Trumpet Against the Monstrous Regiment of Women, 1558.

To promote a woman to rule a nation is unnatural and insulting to God as contrary to his revealed will and law. It is the subversion of good order and justice. No one can deny that it is repugnant to nature that the blind shall lead those who can see, the weak protect the strong, or the foolish and mad govern the discreet and give counsel to those of sober mind. Such are all women compared to man in bearing authority. For as rulers, their sight is blindness; their strength, weakness; their advice, foolishness; and their judgement, frenzy.

Sources D and C suggest that female rule could be a serious problem, whereas Sources A and B do not consider it a serious problem, with Source A more concerned about the question of legitimacy, while Source B does not see female rule as a problem because, according to Mary Tudor, her subjects promised to obey her at her coronation.

The sources are grouped according to their view about the issue in the question.

Source D appears to offer the strongest argument that female rule was a serious problem. Knox argues that female rule was 'unnatural and insulting to God' and subverts 'good order and justice'. Written in 1558 it could be argued that there was some validity to Knox's view as he had experience of the reigns of both Mary Tudor in England and Mary Queen of Scots and neither appeared to have brought stability to their countries. England had witnessed unrest in 1554 with Wyatt's rebellion and Mary Queen of Scots was driven out of Scotland.

The source is evaluated using own knowledge which is accurate and relevant, but not developed excessively.

However, it is unlikely that Knox's view was typical of views in England as many, particularly those of a Protestant or reformist outlook, supported Elizabeth. Moreover, most expected Elizabeth to marry and therefore Knox's concerns in his last sentence that as a ruler her 'sight is blindness', 'strength, weakness', 'advice, foolishness' and 'judgement, frenzy' would not have applied as she would be guided by her husband.

This view is further developed and linked to events in 1558.

Although Source C appears to suggest that female rule could be a serious problem given the need for parliament to pass an Act of Parliament for a marriage treaty between Mary and Philip, it could also be argued that as parliament was able to limit Philip's power in England it was less of an issue. There were obviously concerns about a female ruler being dominated by her husband, particularly a foreigner and one as powerful as Philip, hence the restrictions placed on his power with the queen having 'total control of all offices, lands and revenues, and grant them to natural born Englishmen'. The source also makes it clear that parliament was concerned about being dragged into wars because of the marriage and again took measures to ensure this would not happen. However, despite the treaty, England was drawn into war against France and Spanish influence did become a problem, suggesting that even with the Act female rule was a problem.

There is a balanced discussion about the view of the source in relation to the question.

Precise evidence of England being drawn into the Franco-Habsburg wars is used.

Parliament might impose detailed restrictions, as Source C shows, but the problem was enforcing them. Therefore, although parliament might attempt to impose restrictions, in practice they did not work, suggesting it was a serious problem.

However, Sources A and B are less concerned about the problem of a female ruler. Source A's focus is on the problem of the legitimacy of the ruler. The Devise is more concerned about the legitimacy of Mary and Elizabeth, although it also acknowledges the problems there would be if either came to the throne and married a foreigner as he would 'practise his own country's laws' and 'subvert the commonwealth of this our realm'. However, the source has greater concerns than a female ruler as Lady Jane Grey is put forward as a possible heir, and when the Devise was later altered she was actually named as heir.

The concern of the source is explained in relation to the question and own knowledge is again applied.

However, the source was written either by Northumberland, who had personal reasons to exclude Mary and Elizabeth so as to maintain his influence, or was written by Edward who, for religious reasons, wanted to exclude Mary so that Protestantism would continue. This therefore raises questions about its reliability as its purpose was to justify excluding Mary and Elizabeth. Similarly, Source B does not see female rule as a problem, but the source was written by Mary herself and was designed to rally support for her when she was under threat from Wyatt's rebellion. According to the source female rule was not a problem as not only had the people sworn at her

The provenance of the source is used to challenge the view from earlier in the paragraph.

coronation to 'obey me', but she also argues that 'we shall speedily overthrow these rebels', suggesting that even with a female ruler a rebellion could easily be put down.

Source B also challenges the view in Source D that a woman ruler was the equivalent of the weak leading the strong as in this instance it is Mary who is being strong and disregarding the Council's advice to leave London. There is also some justification in Mary's words as her speech did much to rally support and Wyatt was stopped soon after this speech at the gates of the city, suggesting that one of the concerns about female rulers – namely the problem of dealing with unrest – was unjustified. However, one of the causes of the rebellion was Mary's decision to marry and, as Source C shows, there were problems in having a female ruler as she was expected to marry but there was the problem of who she should marry and limiting their power. •⟵

The sources suggest that there were potential problems of having a female ruler, not simply, as Source D argues, because it was unnatural but because of who they should marry and the powers that the husband would have. However, as Source A suggests, there were other problems, such as legitimacy which were also a concern and probably more so as it allowed Lady Jane to be named as a possible heir. The support there was from many for Elizabeth also suggests that Source D exaggerates the concerns about female rulers. •⟵

> The source is cross-referenced with D, but own knowledge is also used to evaluate it.

> A judgement is reached based on the sources, not own knowledge, and it is briefly supported.

The response is focused on the question of a 'serious problem' and reaches an overall judgement as to whether the sources support the view. The sources are evaluated and own knowledge is used to place them in context and evaluate the views they offer. The response is driven by the sources and their provenance is fully considered in reaching a judgement about their reliability. The response would reach the higher levels.

Characteristics of a good answer

Make a list of the characteristics that make a good answer. Use the example and comments to help you.

Exam focus (AS-level)

Below is a model answer in response to an AS exam-style question and sources. Read the answer and the comments around it.

Use your knowledge of Mary's reign 1553–58 to assess how useful Source C (page 18) is as evidence for the views on a foreign marriage to a female ruler.

The source suggests that, rather than there being problems with the marriage of a female ruler, in this case Mary Tudor, to a foreigner, there are many benefits. The source attempts to address the concerns that because of the sixteenth-century attitude that a wife, even a queen, was subservient to her husband then marriage to a foreigner would lead to them dominating the country. Although the foreign prince will have the 'style and honour of king' and will help administer England, the queen will have total control of offices, lands and revenues. The treaty attempted to address the concerns in England, shown with both the plotting of Wyatt and other rebels once the possibility of marriage became known and the concerns and struggles in Mary's council between Paget and Gardiner, that a foreign marriage would lead to England being dominated by foreigners and that England would become a pawn for the Habsburgs. The source acknowledges some of these concerns as it stresses that England will not become 'entangled in war', although later events that led to the loss of Calais show that this claim was incorrect. There were also concerns about the succession and that Philip might try to take the throne if no heirs resulted from the marriage, but in this instance the treaty was observed and Elizabeth succeeded without difficulties. The source does suggest that England will benefit from the friendship with Spain and, although this was the intention, the death of Mary in 1558 brought the close relationship to an end. The source also attempts to overcome the fears that were present in England that a foreign marriage would lead to patronage being in the hands of foreigners and this was certainly a concern of Wyatt, who had loyally served previous monarchs. There were also rumours circulating in England about the arrival of Spanish troops and the source may be an attempt to address the concerns about the behaviour of the troops and the reduction of England to Spanish servitude.

However, although the source attempts to address the concerns there were in England about the marriage of a female to a foreign ruler, the nature of the source, being an Act of Parliament, means that it will attempt to justify the marriage. The source's purpose was to try to allay the fears there were in England and therefore it will claim that the problems of a foreign marriage, particularly as Mary was determined to marry Philip, were exaggerated and instead would bring the queen support and security, and it will therefore stress the benefits. It will therefore look at only the gains that England, at least in theory, would get from the marriage. Although it addresses some of the concerns, its purpose of reassuring people limits its usefulness as evidence for what would happen in practice. However, it does show how Mary attempted to justify the marriage to her subjects and reassure them.

The source is placed in the context of sixteenth-century attitudes and the concerns that would naturally arise.

Own knowledge is applied directly to the source to explain the concerns and opposition to the marriage, that the treaty was designed to overcome.

Some concerns are developed and knowledge is applied to show that they were justified.

Further concerns that are tackled in the source are explained and knowledge used to explain why these issues needed addressing.

The response deals with the issue of provenance, which it is argued limits its utility.

A judgement as to its utility is developed based on the provenance of the source.

The response addresses the question and considers both the provenance of the source and uses own knowledge to test its utility. Although both elements are discussed and a judgement reached, the provenance could have been further developed in order to explain the limits to the utility of the source and this would also allow the judgement to be further developed. However, all the requirements of the mark scheme have been addressed, at least in part, and therefore the answer would reach a high level.

Reaching a judgement

Rewrite the last paragraph to develop the provenance and judgement in order that the answer would be awarded full marks. Use the mark scheme on page 7 to help you.

2 Religious changes

Religious policies under Edward

Although **Edward** was a minor when he came to the throne, it was soon obvious that he had strong Protestant tendencies. Moves towards Protestantism were made easier by the nature and composition of the **Regency Council** that ran the country. However, support for Protestantism was not particularly strong within the country and there was still a great deal of support for traditional Catholic practices. As a result, moves towards a more reformed religion were quite slow.

Religious change could be split into the following phases during Edward's reign:
- 1547: attack on Catholicism
- 1548: the lack of an official doctrine, but a period of uncontrolled radical Protestant activity
- 1549–52: the establishment of Protestant worship
- 1553: the establishment of a fully reformed Church

The attack on Catholicism, 1547

Somerset's policy was slow and cautious: not only was the country still Catholic, but he was only a moderate Protestant. The bishops were divided and most parish clergy and the population were opposed to change. The government began by examining the condition of the Church through a royal **visitation**. In July 1547 the **Book of Homilies**, giving model sermons, and Erasmus' Paraphrases, were introduced into all churches. Clergy were ordered to conduct services in English and ensure there was an English Bible present and remove superstitious images. **Chantries** were dissolved when parliament met, a further attack on superstition as they were places where masses for the souls of the dead were said. Parliament also repealed the Treason Act which meant radicals were free to discuss more radical reforms as restrictions on what could be said were lifted.

Radical activity, 1548

The abolition of the Treason Act unleashed more radical views and unrest, followed by **iconoclastic attacks** on altars and images. Pamphlets attacking the mass were published. As a result of these development the government had to issue a series of proclamations between January and April 1548 to restore order and limit those who could preach. The impact of these bans was limited as in September 1548 the Council had to ban all public preaching. However, the success of the campaign against the Scots meant that the position of the government was strengthened and therefore more Protestant measures could be brought in during the autumn of 1548.

The establishment of Protestant worship, 1549–52

The Act of Uniformity was passed in January 1549 and this ordered the use of a number of Protestant practices:
- Sacraments were just communion, baptism, confirmation, marriage and burial.
- Clergy could marry.
- Singing for the souls of the dead was ended.
- Holy communion, matins and evensong were in English.
- Laity could take communion in both kinds.

However, some Catholic practices still remained. A new Prayer Book was also brought in and, despite its moderate nature, it created unrest (see pages 24 and 40), but with the fall of Somerset religious change increased in pace: attacks on images were increased, a new **Ordinal** was brought in during January 1550, conservative bishops were removed, a new Treason Act was passed, stone altars were replaced by wooden tables and this was followed by a Second Act of Uniformity.

The establishment of a full reformed Church, 1553

The Second Prayer Book was published and the Act of Uniformity was introduced, which was more Protestant than the first, removed all traces of Catholicism, established Calvin's concept of a spiritual presence and was the basis for all services, but although it was used it did not mean everyone accepted the views. The Forty-Two Articles, outlining doctrine and belief, were drawn up, but never became law because of Edward's death. Therefore, upon Edward's death in 1553, England was legally Protestant.

Add your own knowledge

Below are an exam-style question and Sources A–D. In one colour, draw links between the sources to show ways in which they agree that the Edwardian Reformation was slow and incomplete. In another colour, draw links where they disagree. Around the edge of the sources, write relevant own knowledge. Again, draw links to show the ways in which this agrees or disagrees with the sources.

Using these four sources in their historical context, assess how far they support the view that the Edwardian Reformation was slow and incomplete.

SOURCE A

Thomas Cranmer, author of the Prayer Book, offers a fairly traditional version of communion in the Book of Common Prayer, 1549.

Grant us therefore gracious Lord so to eat the flesh of your dear son Jesus Christ, and to drink his blood, that we may continually dwell in him, and he in us. Amen.

And the minister, delivering the Sacrament of the body of Christ shall say:

The body of our Lord Jesus Christ which is given for you, preserve your body and soul unto everlasting life.

And the minister, delivering the Sacrament of the blood and giving it to everyone to drink, shall say:

The blood of our Lord Jesus Christ which was shed for you, preserve your body and soul unto everlasting life.

SOURCE C

A bishop outlines some measures he wants priests in his diocese to follow, 1552.

You must teach that the salvation of people results from faith in Jesus Christ, not by the merit of good works.

You must condemn the idea of prayers for the dead and worshipping of saints and images.

You must teach that at communion there is no changing of the bread and wine into the body and blood of Jesus Christ.

SOURCE B

Parliament condemns Catholic service books and images, 1550.

The king has issued through parliament a uniform, quietly and goodly order of service called the Book of Common Prayer, which contains nothing but the very pure word of God. However, alongside it are still practised corrupt, untrue and superstitious ceremonies, which allow some to attack the order and meaning of the Prayer Book and encouraged great diversity of opinion. Therefore it is ordered that all books used for the old mass be abolished, and any images of stone, timber or marble be defaced and destroyed.

SOURCE D

Cranmer rewrites the communion service in the 1552 Book of Common Prayer.

Hear us O merciful Father we beg you; and grant that we, receiving these your gifts of bread and wine, according to Christ's example, in remembrance of his death, may share in his most blessed body and blood.

And when the minister delivers the bread, he shall say:

Take and eat this, in remembrance that Christ died for you, and feed on him in your heart by faith, with thanksgiving.

And when the minister delivers the cup, he shall say:

Drink this in remembrance that Christ's blood was shed for you, and be thankful.

Support and opposition for the policies under Edward

Although England was officially Protestant when Edward died in 1553, it did not mean that people actively supported the religious changes of **Somerset** and **Northumberland**. Moreover, England was still Catholic when Henry died in 1547 and it is unlikely that the religious beliefs of the English people would have been changed by 1553.

The extent of change

Legislation, such as the Second Act of Uniformity and the Second Prayer Book, that made England a fully Protestant country was brought in only during the last year of Edward's reign so had little time to have an impact, while the Forty-Two Articles never became law.

Despite these problems, many churchwarden accounts suggest that the reforms had been carried out, altars had been replaced and the new service books were being used. However, imposing the changes was not easy and this is shown by the legislation to remove images:

- July 1547: **royal injunctions** ordered the removal of superstitious images.
- February 1548: all images to be removed.
- December 1548: proclamation orders all remaining images to be destroyed.

The amount of legislation needed suggests that even this task was not straightforward.

Religious unrest

It is difficult to argue against the view that the Western rebellion of 1549 in Devon and Cornwall was religiously motivated. Most of the demands were religious and the rising had begun in Devon at Sampford Courtenay in June 1549, when the parishioners had demanded that the priest used the old Prayer Book and not the new to say mass. The rebels demanded:

- the restoration of the Six Articles
- mass in Latin
- holy bread and water, palms and ashes all to be restored
- images to be restored
- prayers for the souls of the dead.

The demands were dominated by the insistence that traditional practices were restored, although there was no demand for the restoration of papal authority.

However, it was not just in the West Country that there was religious unrest. The rising in Yorkshire at Seamer was largely triggered by religious grievances, as was unrest in Oxfordshire and Hampshire. However, Kett's rebellion in East Anglia wanted the religious changes to go at a faster pace.

The evidence of wills

Although evidence from wills is difficult to interpret, it appears that they show little support for the changes except in London, the south-east and East Anglia. Yet even in Kent preambles to wills showed that only 8 per cent were Protestant in 1549; this was slightly more in Suffolk, with 27 per cent for the whole of Edward's reign. But this can be contrasted with York and the south-west. In York there were just two before 1550 and one in the south-west, suggesting that traditional religion still had much appeal, which would also make Mary's task that much easier.

Local reactions

Although the evidence of wills suggests little support for the reformed faith, there were some parishes where changes were welcomed, and it is unlikely that the new Prayer Book had no impact. However, the amount of change had probably left many confused or indifferent, with many simply conforming because they were told they had to. This also appears to be the case with many clergy, who served Henry, Edward and Mary.

Spot the inference

High-level answers avoid just summarising or paraphrasing the sources, and instead make inferences from the sources. Below are a source and a series of statements. Read the source and decide which of the statements:

- makes an inference from the source (I)
- paraphrases the source (P)
- summarises the source (S)
- cannot be justified from the source (X).

How useful is the source as evidence of the difficulties of introducing religious reform?

		I	P	S	X
1	The main reasons why the introduction of Protestantism was slow were the lack of qualified clergy and legislation				
2	It would be difficult to make England a Protestant nation within a short period and everything possible needs to be done to encourage the government				
3	There were moves towards Protestantism, encouraged by the government, who considered religious change a priority				
4	Bucer is concerned that not only can the bishops not agree on doctrine, but there is a lack of qualified clergy who do little to help by reading services quickly; the bishops state that they need parliamentary support to act but parliament has many other issues that need its attention				

SOURCE

Martin Bucer, a German Protestant who arrived in England in 1548 and taught theology at Cambridge University, sends news of religious events in England to a leading European Protestant, John Calvin, in June 1550.

The bishops have not yet agreed on Christian doctrine, let alone rules of the Church, and very few parishes have qualified clergymen. Sometimes the clergy read the services rapidly, so that ordinary people have no more understanding of it than if it were still in Latin rather than English. When these problems are presented to the bishops, they say they cannot correct them without an Act of Parliament. Though parliament meets every year, the number of secular matters stops Church affairs being discussed. When you next write to the Duke of Somerset, you must urge him to reform the Church.

Using provenance and own knowledge

Read the source above and consider the following question:

How useful is the source as evidence for the difficulties of introducing religious reform?

- In using provenance to evaluate the source, who is it being written to, why would it be written, how might that affect its utility?
- In using own knowledge to evaluate the source, what was important about the circumstances in which the letter was written?

Recommended reading

Below is a list of suggested further reading on this topic.
- *England 1485–1603*, pages 123–30, Mary Dicken and Nicholas Fellows (2015)
- *English Reformations*, pages 168–203, Christopher Haigh (1993)
- *The Early Tudors*, pages 209–25, David Rogerson, Samantha Ellsmore and David Hudson (2001)
- *Henry VII to Mary I, 1485–1558*, pages 146–53, Roger Turvey (2015)

Religious policies under Mary

At the start of her reign Mary issued a proclamation stating that she intended to proceed cautiously in religious matters, but few had doubts as to what her aims were, which were to:
- undo the religious changes made since 1529
- restore papal authority
- restore traditional Catholic practices
- re-establish monasteries
- end clerical marriage
- persecute those who did not agree with her views
- secure a long-term future for Catholicism by marrying and having an heir.

She was welcomed with enthusiasm, bells were rung and parliament opened with a mass even though it was illegal. Despite this apparent support, there were a number of difficulties, with **Gardiner** uncertain about restoring papal authority, Renard about restoring monasteries and the Pope that she would move too quickly.

Restoration of papal authority

Parliament met in October 1553, but refused to repeal the Act of Supremacy. However, it did pass an Act of Repeal which undid the changes made under Edward and restored the situation to that of 1547 under the Act of Six Articles. Mary used the **royal prerogative** to suspend the Second Act of Uniformity and restored mass, which did not provoke serious opposition. However, there was some disquiet, as seen with Wyatt's rebellion (see page 44), which happened before any significant religious changes had occurred.

Restoration of Catholic practices

In the spring of 1554 royal injunctions restored some traditional Catholic practices, such as **Holy Days**, processions and ceremonies. A large number of married clergy were also **deprived** and Protestant bishops were removed.

The heresy laws and the Second Act of Repeal

Initial attempts to restore the heresy laws in April were rejected by parliament. They would not agree to this until guarantees were given that former monastic lands would not be restored. However, opposition was probably due more to factional conflict (see page 16) than opposition to Mary's religious policies as they were passed a few months later.

The Second Act of Repeal, which repealed all religious legislation passed since 1529, was passed in November 1554, but Mary was forced into a compromise with landowners, guaranteeing the rights of those who had bought church land since 1536.

The heresy laws were reintroduced in 1554 and burnings started in February 1555 (see page 30).

Catholic reform

The return of **Pole** to England was followed by the introduction of a number of positive measures to increase the appeal of Catholicism:
- Bishops were ordered to make regular visitations and check clerical behaviour.
- The London **Synod**, which stressed the importance of priests being resident and the ending of **pluralism**, was established.
- Pole ordered new publications, including a Catholic New Testament and Book of Homilies.
- He wanted **seminaries** in every diocese.

There were also attempts to control Protestant literature and increase the availability of Catholic works, with the sponsoring of sermons at St Paul's Cross and the publication of writings by writers such as Matthew Hogarde.

Doing reliability well

Below are an exam-style question, a set of definitions listing common reasons why sources can be unreliable and Sources A–D. For each source, write a critical account of whether it is a reliable or unreliable piece of evidence, justifying your answer by referring to the definitions below.

Using these four sources in their historical context, assess how far they support the view that the religious policies of Mary's reign were based mainly on reconciliation.

- **Vested interest**: the source is written so that the writer can protect their own power or interests.
- **Second-hand report**: the writer is not in a position to know and is relying on someone else's information.
- **Expertise**: the source is written on a subject that the author is an expert in.
- **Political bias**: the source is written by a politician and it reflects their political views.
- **Reputation**: the source is written to protect the writer's reputation.

Source A is reliable/unreliable as evidence for Mary's religious aims because:

_____

Source B is reliable/unreliable as evidence for Mary's religious aims because:

_____

Source C is reliable/unreliable as evidence for Mary's religious aims because:

_____

Source D is reliable/unreliable as evidence for Mary's religious aims because:

_____

SOURCE A

Mary reassures her subjects about her religious aims in a royal proclamation, 1553.

The queen, being by the goodness of God settled in her just possession of the crown of this realm, cannot hide that religion which God and the world know she has always professed. The queen desires the same religion to be quietly and charitably embraced by all her subjects. And yet she intends not to compel any of her subjects to attend Catholic services until such time as further decision, by common consent, may be taken. She therefore wills and commands all her good loving subjects to live together in Christian charity.

SOURCE B

The Spanish ambassador comments on lay people owning former church lands in a letter, 8 August 1554.

The present possessors must be reassured that they will not have to hand back these lands. Otherwise we shall never achieve the desired result. Unless Cardinal Pole takes this advice he will run great risks himself and make the whole religious question much more difficult.

SOURCE C

The imperial ambassador comments on events after Pole's arrival, 30 November 1554.

Last Sunday the Dean of St Paul's cathedral preached a sermon about the return of lands to the Church. It was disliked since he argued that the lay owners of former church lands should now return them, even though they had obtained permission to own them. There was a general opinion that Cardinal Pole had put the Dean up to this, but as the Dean had been sent for and reprimanded by the Council, it seems he must have acted without the knowledge of the Council or the Cardinal. The Cardinal has behaved well so far and followed your Majesty's advice.

SOURCE D

A Protestant clergyman writing in Elizabeth I's reign describes the execution of the vicar of Hadleigh, in Suffolk. From John Foxe, The Book of Martyrs, published 1563.

The streets of Hadleigh were crowded on both sides. Dr Taylor's hair had been clipped, on the orders of Bishop Bonner. Holmes, yeoman of the guard, gave Dr Taylor a heavy blow on the head. Then the doctor knelt down and prayed and when he had prayed he went to the stake and kissed it. Then they bound him with chains. At last they kindled the fires. So he stood still until the man Soyce, with a weapon, struck him on the head and the corpse fell into the fire.

Attitudes to Marian policies and Catholic restoration

The reaction to the crowning of **Lady Jane Grey** and Mary's overthrow of her, as well as the lack of evidence for popular support for many of the Edwardian reforms, suggests that traditional religious practices were still popular. However, as the 1549 Western rebellion had shown, that does not mean there was unconditional support for the restoration of papal authority. Moreover, some of the support for Mary was not because of her religion, but because she was seen as the rightful ruler.

Evidence for popular support for Mary's religious policies

Mary's return to London was greeted with joy, bells were rung and parliament opened with a sung mass even though it was still illegal. In Oxford **chalices** reappeared and an altar and cross were set up on 23 August at St Nicholas Cole Abbey in London, where mass was said – a practice that was copied the next day in other churches in the capital. Large numbers also turned out for Mary's coronation, in stark contrast to Lady Jane Grey's. This reaction may have convinced Mary that the restoration of Catholicism would be easy.

Opposition in parliament

Although there was opposition in parliament to some religious changes (see page 24), this was usually not the result of religious concerns, as was the case with the heresy laws, the Aliens Act or the Second Act of Repeal, but due to factional, economic and land concerns, particularly the possibility of the loss of monastic lands which many gentry and nobility had purchased since 1536. Once they had guarantees about their security the legislation was passed.

Wyatt's rebellion

Wyatt's rebellion is sometimes seen as evidence of the unpopularity of Mary's religious policies, but it began before any serious changes had been implemented and, although the leaders had Protestant sympathies, was probably due more to Mary's proposed marriage to Philip of Spain than religious reasons, although the two were closely linked in the popular mind. The marriage could also strengthen Mary's position and make it easier for her to impose religious legislation, and even secure a Catholic succession, although given that Mary was already 37 that was perhaps less likely.

The Marian exiles

As the nature of the religious changes became apparent in the early months of 1554, some Protestants began to leave England. In total some 800 committed Protestants, mostly gentry, clergy and wealthier individuals, left England and went into exile on the continent for the rest of Mary's reign. However, this was not really an option for the less well-off. Moreover, at the start of Mary's reign, many were willing to wait and see what developments took place, with a number, correctly as it turned out, not expecting Mary's reign to be long given her age, which also raised doubts about her ability to produce an heir.

Popular support

This is seen in parishes, such as Morebath in Devon, where parishioners raised considerable sums of money to purchase **vestments** and other equipment needed to carry out Catholic services. Evidence would suggest that Catholic worship returned speedily to most parishes. However, some churches had been badly neglected during Edward's reign and it would take time to restore all the equipment. Yet, it was not this that was the greatest obstacle to a Catholic restoration, but Mary's failure to produce an heir. The problems that Elizabeth would have in establishing a Protestant Church is clear evidence of how popular most of Mary's policies actually were.

Explain the differences by using provenance

1 What does Source A show about Parkyn's view of Mary's religious policies?
2 Why was the book written?
3 What was happening when the book was written?
4 What does Source B show about Hickman's view of Mary's religious policies?
5 Why was it written?
6 What was happening when she was writing?

SOURCE A

A Yorkshire priest records reactions of the clergy to the restoration of Roman Catholic services at the start of Mary's reign. From Robert Parkyn, Narrative of the Reformation, 1553.

In August, Queen Mary issued a proclamation licensing priests to say mass in Latin after the ancient custom used in her father's day. Then the holy church began to rejoice, singing praise to God with heart and tongue. But many heretics did not rejoice at all. It was a joy to hear and see those sinful priests who had lived their lives immorally with their whores look so dismayed. They were commanded to forsake their mistresses and do open penance according to the canon law, which then took effect.

SOURCE B

A committed Protestant and wife of a wealthy merchant recalls her experiences early in Mary's reign, writing in old age under Elizabeth. From Rose Hickman, Memoir of Protestant Life under Mary I, 1610.

When Queen Mary came to the crown, the idolatrous mass was established and cruel persecution began of good Christians who refused to accept popery. We sheltered many in our house in London. My husband smuggled some of these good Christians overseas, helping them with money. When it was proclaimed that everyone should receive the popish sacrament, I went to the bishops who were imprisoned in Oxford and later martyred, to ask whether my child should be baptised by the popish ritual. They said that he could, but advised me rather to go overseas. Afterwards I left for Antwerp.

 Using your own knowledge

In order to find evidence for a possible source-based question on the popularity of Mary's religious policies, write two extended paragraphs using your own knowledge and material from this chapter.

- Paragraph 1 will show the popularity of Mary's religious policies and include four examples of popularity.
- Paragraph 2 will show the unpopularity of Mary's religious policies and include four examples of the lack of popularity.

Catholic persecution

It is the reintroduction of the heresy laws that is the most remembered policy of Mary, reflected in her nickname of 'Bloody Mary'. During the period from the first burning, that of John Rogers in February 1555, nearly 300 went to the stake, of whom 51 were women, with most of the burnings in the south-east, London, Canterbury and Colchester. According to some accounts it lost Mary support as many, such as the fisherman Rawlins White, were ordinary citizens. However, views have been coloured by the writings of the Protestant, John Foxe, writing during Elizabeth's reign.

John Foxe and his impact

The burnings are largely remembered because of John Foxe's *Acts and Monuments* (1563), more commonly known as *The Book of Martyrs*. It is this that has influenced the understanding and impact of the events, suggesting that there was widespread opposition to the regime and that it was the fires of Smithfield that turned England Protestant. Some have argued that those who actually attended the burnings were so impressed by the dedication of those being burnt that they themselves converted. However, evidence to support this claim is limited and only one person appears to have been so moved as to convert.

The impact of the burnings

Historians have also challenged Foxe's view, even though the Spanish ambassador expressed concern about the impact and feared it would cause unrest.

In October 1555 the bishops Ridley and Latimer were burnt at Oxford and this was followed in March 1556 by the burning of **Thomas Cranmer**. Although for Mary the burning of the man who had ended her mother's marriage to Henry and supported Lady Jane Grey might be seen as necessary, some have argued it was her biggest error. Cranmer had committed treason in supporting Lady Jane Grey and could have been executed: his burning gave him the chance to withdraw his previous recantations once it was apparent he would not be spared and such was his courage that his burning did not help the Catholic cause.

The death of Gardiner in November 1555 removed a restraining influence on Mary. Initially he had supported the persecutions, but he became aware that they were not working and might be hardening opposition and his death was followed by an increase, with some 274 perishing in the last three years of her reign.

However, although large numbers attended the burnings they were usually seen as spectacles. Some, such as the cherry pickers from Kent, even welcomed them as it gave them an increased market to which they could sell their produce. Although London magistrates had to order the burnings to take place early in the day so that the numbers attending were reduced, this is probably because of the disruption that London apprentices caused at many events, rather than support for the victims. It should also be remembered that the prosecutions occurred only because the victims had been reported and local authorities were willing to enforce the law.

The geography of the burnings

Most took place in the south-east, because that was where most Protestants were. However, it might also be because the area was closer to London and the authorities were more concerned about the dangers and put increased pressure on local authorities to act, whereas areas further away from the capital were less susceptible to such influence. This view is supported by the number of letters sent to **Justices of the Peace (JPs)** in the south urging action. Some have argued that the need for such letters is evidence they were unwilling to support the action, but other factors may also explain the delays:
- War against France in 1557.
- They were unwilling to enforce other legislation, such as the Vagrancy Laws.
- There were regular reminders to JPs to implement laws.

It is difficult to determine the impact of the burnings. The degree of damage it did to Mary's popularity is debatable. It was not a success but probably not a disaster.

Mind map

Using the information from the opposite page and your own knowledge, create a mind map that considers the scale and reaction to the Marian persecutions. Did they achieve their aim?

Add your own knowledge

Below are a question and Sources A–D. In one colour, draw links between the sources to show ways in which they agree about whether the restoration of Catholicism had made much progress by the time of Mary's death. In another colour, draw links to show how they disagree. Around the edge of the source, write relevant own knowledge using the mind map, your own knowledge and information from the page opposite.

Using these sources in their historical context, assess how far they support the view that Mary's restoration of Catholicism had made little progress by her death in 1558.

SOURCE A

The imperial ambassador describes parliament's reaction to Cardinal Pole's speech on his arrival in England in November 1554.

Yesterday, parliament came to the unanimous decision that all the laws and statutes contrary to the Pope's authority should be repealed, the Church's authority be once more acknowledged, and the Cardinal admitted as Legate to carry out his mission. Although about 500 persons were gathered together, there was only one opposing voice, and there was no hint of making conditions about Church property.

SOURCE B

The imperial ambassador comments on the reaction in London to the burnings, February 1555.

The people of London are murmuring about the cruel enforcement of the recent Acts of Parliament against heresy which has now begun, as shown publicly when a certain Rogers was burnt yesterday. Some of the onlookers wept. Others prayed to God to give them strength, persistence, and patience to bear the pain and not to convert back to Catholicism. Others gathered up the ashes and bones and wrapped them up in paper to preserve them. Yet others threatened the bishops. The haste with which the bishops have proceeded in this matter may well cause a revolt.

SOURCE C

An Elizabethan Protestant writer describes the burning of the vicar of Hadleigh, Suffolk. From John Foxe, Acts and Monuments *(The Book of Martyrs), 1563.*

Taylor was brought to Hadleigh bridge, where a poor man with five children stood. They held up their hands and he said, 'O dear father and good shepherd, Dr Taylor, God help you, just as you have often helped me and my poor children!' The streets were full on both sides with men and women of the town and country who wanted to see and bless him. When they saw his reverend and ancient face, with a long white beard, they wept and cried out 'God save you, good Dr Taylor!'

SOURCE D

The officials of churches in the diocese of Canterbury are ordered to fit out their churches for Catholic worship, 1557.

Goodnestone Church:

To provide front cloths for the altar for holy days, a canopy and veil for Lent.

To make a new lock for the font.

Goodhurst Church:

To provide two decent banners before Rogation week. To repair the chancel ceiling, and the glass windows of the church.

Exam focus (A-level)

Below is a model answer in response to an exam-style A-level question and source. Read the answer and the comments around it.

Using these four sources in their historical context, assess the view that the restoration of Catholicism in 1553–58 enjoyed little popular support.

SOURCE A

A Yorkshire priest records reactions of the clergy to the restoration of Roman Catholic services at the start of Mary's reign. From Robert Parkyn, Narrative of the Reformation, 1532–54.

From August 1553 in many places in Yorkshire, priests were very glad to say mass in Latin, according to the fervent zeal and love they had unto God and his laws. Holy bread and water was given, altars were rebuilt, pictures and images set up once more. The English service was voluntarily laid aside and the Latin taken up again, and all without compulsion of any Act or law, but merely on the wish of Queen Mary. And all the old ceremonies were used regularly, once the Lord Cardinal Pole arrived in this realm in November 1554.

SOURCE B

The accounts kept by the churchwardens of a Berkshire parish record the impact of the Marian restoration in the south of England.

1553 Payment to the stonemason for setting up again the high altar.

1554 Payment to Henry Snodman to remove a table which served in the church for the communion in the wicked time of schism.

1555 Payment to Edward Whayne for mending the clergyman's robes.

1556 Payment to attend the church inspection of my Lord Cardinal Pole. Payment in Abingdon for buying images. Payment for writing an answer to certain questions concerning Religion circulated by my Lord Cardinal Pole to certain of the clergy and Justices of the Peace.

SOURCE C

A committed Protestant and wife of a wealthy merchant recalls her experiences early in Mary's reign, writing in old age under Elizabeth. From Rose Hickman, Memoir of Protestant Life under Mary I, 1610.

When Queen Mary came to the crown, the idolatrous mass was established and cruel persecution began of good Christians who refused to accept popery. We sheltered many in our house in London. My husband smuggled some of these good Christians overseas, helping them with money. When it was proclaimed that everyone should receive the popish sacrament, I went to the bishops who were imprisoned in Oxford and later martyred, to ask whether my child should be baptised by the popish ritual. They said that he could, but advised me rather to go overseas. Afterwards I left for Antwerp.

SOURCE D

The imperial ambassador comments on the reaction in London to the burnings, February 1555.

The people of London are murmuring about the cruel enforcement of the recent Acts of Parliament against heresy which has now begun, as shown publicly when a certain Rogers was burnt yesterday. Some of the onlookers wept. Others prayed to God to give them strength, persistence, and patience to bear the pain and not to convert back to Catholicism. Others gathered up the ashes and bones and wrapped them up in paper to preserve them. Yet others threatened the bishops. The haste with which the bishops have proceeded in this matter may well cause a revolt. If the people got the upper hand, not only would the cause of religion be again threatened, but the persons of your majesty and the queen might be in peril.

Sources A and B appear to challenge the view that the restoration of Catholicism enjoyed little popular support, while Sources C and D suggest that there was both opposition and the fear of unrest because of some of the policies pursued by Mary's government. However, the nature of some of the sources suggests that such a view might be simplistic and the restoration enjoyed popular support.

The sources are usefully grouped together to give a structure to the answer.

Source A argues that not only was the restoration of Catholicism quick, but it was also popular as 'the English service was voluntarily laid aside and the Latin taken up again, and all without compulsion', not only that but all the old ceremonies were being used by the end of 1554 – just over a year after Mary's accession. Although Parkyn's account is based on the north of England, where Catholicism had been traditionally strong as was seen in the reaction to the closure of the smaller monasteries in 1536 and the formula of wills under both Henry and Edward, evidence from Melton Mowbray where the bells were rung to greet Mary's accession or in parliament where a mass was said before it was law suggest that his account was not untypical, even though he was a firm supporter of Catholicism. This is further reinforced by the restoration of images and pictures, as well as altars being rebuilt and while his account shows that this was in the north of England, evidence from Morebath in the West Country and from Source B would reinforce such a view, even if it was slower in the south. It should also be remembered that this was quite a remarkable achievement given the cost of the restoration of many of these items, although there is also evidence that some had been hidden during Edward's reign so were readily available when Mary came to the throne, further supporting the view that people welcomed her coming to the throne knowing that she would restore Catholicism.

Source A is thoroughly evaluated in relation to the question. Detailed own knowledge is directly applied to the source and the issue of provenance is also considered. The link with B helps to reinforce the point that it was not just in the north that restoration occurred.

Source B adds to this view and shows that the restoration of Catholic items, even in a parish in the south of England, where Protestantism might be stronger, still took place. However, the process was slower here and, with Source A, might suggest there was some regional variation, but again given the cost of restoring some of the items listed, such as images, progress within the first three years of Mary's reign was still encouraging. Although the source is a simple account of the money spent by the Church to restore Catholic ritual, there is the suggestion that it was also sympathetic to the restoration as it refers to the earlier period as that 'wicked time of schism', which, if it is an accurate indication of the views in the south of England, suggests the restoration was popular. This is further supported by evidence from wills in the south, which show only 20 per cent of London wills at the end of Edward's reign having a Protestant direction, further supporting the argument that Catholicism was still popular.

The link between B and A is further developed to reinforce the point and provide a picture across the country. However, as with A, B is considered in a balanced manner, with acknowledgement that the process was slower.

This view is, however, challenged to some extent by Sources C and D. Source C certainly suggests that there was opposition to Catholicism as people fled the country because of its restoration. While some 800 did go into exile that figure does not suggest great unpopularity, although it must be remembered that only the wealthy would be able to afford the option. Hickman does also suggest that there were some clergy who supported Protestantism, but this source was written by a devout Protestant who was not only concerned about having her child baptised by a Catholic priest, but herself went into exile, suggesting her view of events may not be representative of most. She is also looking back during Elizabeth's reign at events under Mary and may therefore view them rather differently, contrasting the triumph of the reformed religion under Elizabeth with the bad days of Mary and her 'idolatrous mass'.

However, Source D appears to reinforce the view that there was opposition and the restoration was unwelcome and according to the imperial ambassador was bringing England close to revolt. Despite Renard's view that the burnings were causing opposition, there is actually little evidence to support his claim and he may well be exaggerating the issue to try to persuade Philip to return to England, particularly as Philip had already cautioned Mary about the implementation of the heresy laws. As ambassador, Renard's knowledge of events outside the capital would also have been limited and therefore, while there might be some truth that people murmured in London, there is no evidence of serious unrest at the burnings. It is true that in London the burnings had to take place early in the morning because of fears of unrest from the London apprentices, but they were often causing trouble and their activities should not be seen as an indicator that there was unpopularity. It should also be remembered that, despite Renard's comments, the only reason anyone was burnt was because they had been reported and prosecuted, further evidence that there were people who were willing to inform against the religious beliefs of their neighbours, further evidence that the informers supported the Catholic faith. Renard also suggests that there were Protestants present who encouraged those being burnt to remain strong in their faith, and while that might be true, there were also many more who attended the burnings as entertainment – certainly the Kent cherry growers made large sums of money selling their wares at the events, difficult as that might be to understand today. It should also be remembered that the heresy laws had been passed by parliament, further suggesting that Renard's view about the unpopularity of the measure is unfounded.

Although Sources C and D suggest that there was opposition, the nature of the sources raises doubts about such a claim and, although some opposed the policy, the numbers were limited. Sources A and B offer a more accurate view of the reaction to the restoration and this is further supported by the welcome given to Mary in 1553 and the problems Elizabeth I would face from 1558 onwards in implementing a Protestant settlement both within parliament and the country.

A link between the two sources is made.

Own knowledge is used to test the provenance.

There is an impressive level of own knowledge used to test the view in the source.

Sources C and D are treated together. The question of the provenance of both is considered and knowledge is also applied to explain the limitations of both sources in terms of the question.

The judgement is based on the sources and this is supported by some brief but relevant contextual own knowledge.

The response is focused on the question and, although the sources are treated discretely, there is some cross-referencing which is used effectively to take the argument forward. The sources are all evaluated using both provenance and own knowledge, with some of the own knowledge being quite detailed, but it is used and linked to the actual source under discussion and not simply imparted. The judgement is based on the sources and therefore, given both provenance and own knowledge are used effectively, the response will reach the higher levels.

> **Using own knowledge and the source**
>
> In different colours, underline examples where the answer uses own knowledge, evaluates, cross-references and quotes from the sources.

Exam focus (AS-level)

REVISED ☐

Read source E and answer the following question.

Use your knowledge of religious changes under Mary to assess how useful the source is as evidence of opposition to Mary I's religious policies.

SOURCE E

A royal messenger, and cousin of a former Lord Chancellor, records an eyewitness account of an event in London. From Charles Wriothesley's Chronicle of England *for April 1554.*

On Sunday a villainous event took place in Cheapside. A dead cat was hanged on the post of gallows, dressed in cloth like the vestment of a priest at mass with crosses front and back. Its head was shaved, a bottle was nearby and between its front paws was a piece of paper like a consecrated wafer. It was taken to bishop Bonner of London, who showed it to the audience attending the sermon at St Paul's Cross. The Lord Mayor offered a reward to anyone naming the culprit. Inquiries were made and several persons were imprisoned under suspicion.

3 Rebellion and unrest

Causes of the unrest, 1547–58

REVISED

The period from the death of Henry VIII in 1547 to the death of **Mary Tudor** in 1558 witnessed a large number of rebellions, and an even greater number of local riots and smaller outbreaks of unrest. There were a number of causes of the unrest.

Social and economic problems

Social and economic issues were often an underlying cause of the unrest and included issues such as:

- population growth
- rising prices
- poor harvests
- increasing poverty
- **enclosure**.

However, although these problems were becoming more acute, they were seldom the trigger for unrest (see page 38). Nevertheless, some of the issues, particularly enclosure, did play a significant role in the outbreak of Kett's rebellion in 1549 and had started earlier unrest at Northaw in Hertfordshire in 1548 (see page 40). The issue of enclosure led to the establishment of an **Enclosure Commission** by Somerset and this convinced many peasants that he was sympathetic to their cause and may have encouraged the unrest in the summer of 1549 that gripped much of central and southern England.

Factional and political causes

The accession of a minor, **Edward VI**, increased factional conflicts within government. As Edward was only a minor it meant that the government was in the hands of a group of councillors, or the **Regency Council**. Members of the Council looked to increase their influence and also sought to increase their personal wealth. This was seen in the struggle in 1549 and the early months of 1550 when **Somerset** was removed from power by a coup and **Northumberland** succeeded him and became Lord President of the Council. The factional struggle continued; Somerset attempted to regain his influence until he was executed in 1552.

This was not the end of the political struggles as Northumberland attempted to retain influence upon the death of Edward VI in 1553 by placing **Lady Jane Grey** on the throne, which brought England close to civil war (see page 42), and then after the defeat of this coup, Mary Tudor's reign also witnessed factional conflict. There were attempts by some councillors to dissuade Mary from marrying Philip of Spain as they feared losing influence to Spaniards and this encouraged Wyatt's rebellion of 1554 (see page 44). It can therefore be seen that the presence of both a minor and then a woman on the throne contributed to unrest.

Religious change

Religious uncertainty caused by the changes under Henry VIII added to the potential for instability. This was first seen in 1547 and 1548 in Cornwall when William Body attempted to supervise the destruction of images. The introduction of a new Prayer Book in 1549 led to the Western or Prayer Book rebellion in 1549 as people in the West Country complained about the abolition of traditional religious practices and even Kett's rebels had some religious grievances. However, unlike the Western rebels, their demands were for further moves towards Protestantism, rather than its abandonment.

The potential restoration of Catholicism by Mary may have played a role in Northumberland's decision to try to put the Protestant Lady Jane Grey on the throne and similarly Wyatt may have rebelled because he did not want a Catholic regime. However, there is more evidence to suggest that these rebellions were more factional and political in nature.

Spot the inference

a

High-level answers avoid just summarising or paraphrasing the sources, and instead make inferences from the sources. Below are a source and a series of statements. Read Source A and decide which of the statements:

- makes an inference from the source (I)
- paraphrases the source (P)
- summarises the source (S)
- cannot be justified from the source (X).

How useful is Source A as evidence for the causes of unrest in England in 1549?

		I	P	S	X
1	The risings have spread and could be a threat. The demands of the rebels are largely social and economic, with some unrealistic requests, but where handled well they can be put down quickly so are not a serious threat.				
2	The ambassador is saying that peasant revolts have spread to all parts of England. He says that the peasants want land to be leased to them at the same rate as it was under Henry VII. The riots in some areas ended when food was taxed at a reasonable price. He says religion is not a major cause of the unrest.				
3	The revolts are widespread and are caused by economic issues, such as rent and the taxes on foodstuffs, while religion is not a major cause. Some ended when the taxes on food were reduced.				
4	The revolts were less about social and economic issues and more about religion and political problems.				

SOURCE A

An ambassador writes an account of the risings of 1549.

The revolt of the peasants has increased and spread, so that now they have risen in every part of England, asking for things just and unjust. They demand they may use the land that once used to be public property, and that land leased to them shall be considered to be of the same value now as in the time of Henry VII, who died in 1509. This last request is very difficult to meet. In Kent and Essex the risings ended when foodstuffs were taxed at a reasonable price. There is no mention of religion made among any of them, except in Cornwall and Norfolk.

Assessing reliability

a

How reliable is Source A as an expression of the causes of unrest in England in 1549?

To help you decide, complete the table below.

When was it written?	
Why would the ambassador be eager to report the unrest in England?	
Was it a private or a public document?	
Who would read the document?	
From your own knowledge, was this typical of the explanations given for the unrest in England?	

Social and economic developments

The economic and social changes that affected England in the sixteenth century, particularly in the middle of the century, have often been seen by historians to be the underlying cause of the unrest that appeared to grip the mid Tudor period. However, many contemporaries saw the social and economic problems in more moralistic terms, often blaming landowners for being greedy.

Population rise

Contemporary writings ignored the most important underlying issue, the rise in population. For the first time since the **Black Death** in the fourteenth century, the population was rising. Although there are no accurate figures available, it would appear that between 1525 and 1551 it rose from 2.3 million to 3 million. This may not appear large, but it had a far reaching impact. Agricultural productivity was unable to keep pace with the rise and therefore the price of food rose and this meant that when there were bad harvests, of which there were many in the period, it became a serious issue. Grain prices rose faster than other food prices and because it was the staple diet it had an even greater impact.

Not only did the population rise, but the structure changed. It was a young population, which meant that many were too young to work, and therefore the dependency ratio increased as many were children who were consumers but not producers.

Agricultural problems and enclosure

Not only was it difficult to increase production levels of grain, as people at the time did not have fertilisers, nor were they aware of crop rotation, but many farmers were also changing from arable to sheep farming as the demand for cloth grew. This created further problems as sheep farming required fewer labourers, and therefore caused unemployment.

It also encouraged another development, which was seen as an evil by many contemporary commentators: enclosure. The government of Somerset attempted to tackle the problem by establishing Enclosure Commissions in both 1548 and 1549 to look into the problem, but attempts at legislation were blocked by the gentry in parliament as they were gaining from such developments. Somerset issued proclamations to try to force landowners to reverse the development, but this lost him the support of the gentry and encouraged the lower orders to take action themselves and throw down hedges.

Price rise

Contemporaries tended to blame the rise in prices on the greed of landowners, but it was largely due to the rising population and the inability of the agricultural system to meet the growing demand for food.

Year	Price compared to 1508 (%)
1508	100
1520	137
1530	169
1545	191
1546	248
1549	214

The situation was made worse by the **debasement** of the currency to finance the wars against France and Scotland in the 1540s. It meant more money was in circulation but not more food and therefore prices rose further. This was made worse by bad harvests, with six bad harvests in the period from 1547 to 1558, and those in 1548 and 1549 were little better. The poor suffered even more because the **Dissolution of the Monasteries** had removed the one institution that helped during difficult times.

Poverty and vagrancy

Enclosure had decreased the numbers needed in the workforce and a slump in the cloth trade only added to unemployment. The price rise also meant there was an increase in the number of poor and this worried the authorities, particularly when large numbers were concentrated together, as they lacked a force to maintain order and prevent crime. The government therefore brought in harsh measures, such as the 1547 Vagrancy Act, which condemned vagrants to slavery.

Add your own knowledge

Below are an exam-style question and Sources A–D. In one colour, draw links between the sources to show ways in which they agree. In another colour, draw links where they disagree. Around the edge of the sources, write relevant own knowledge. Again, draw links to show the ways in which this agrees or disagrees with the sources.

Using these sources in their historical context, assess the view that the price rise was the main reason for the social problems in this period.

SOURCE A

A social commentator attacks the rise of oppressive landlords. From 'A Supplication of the Poor Commons', 1546.

Many landlords oppress the common people. They have increased their rents, so that they charge £40 rather than £2 for a new lease, and £5 not 5 nobles (almost £2) for its annual rent, so we now pay more to them than we earn. The result is that many thousands of us who once lived honestly upon our labour must now beg, or borrow, or rob and steal, to get food for our poor wives and children. They also compel others to surrender their rights to hold leases for two or three lives and to accept instead leases for just twenty-one years.

SOURCE B

A clergyman identifies some major economic grievances. From Thomas Becon, The Jewel of Joy, *1547–48.*

See how rich men, especially sheep owners, oppress the king's subjects by enclosing the common pasture and filling it with their sheep. How many sheep they have! Yet when was wool so expensive, or mutton so great a price? If this goes on, the people will die of cold or starve to death. For these greedy wolves will either sell their wool and their sheep at their own high price, or else not at all. Other men buy up houses, even whole villages, and then allow them to fall into ruin and decay.

SOURCE C

An ambassador writes an account of the risings.

The revolt of the peasants has increased and spread, so that now they have risen in every part of England, asking for things just and unjust. They demand they may use the land that once used to be public property, and that land leased to them shall be considered to be of the same value now as in the time of Henry VII, who died in 1509. This last request is very difficult to meet. In Kent and Essex the risings ended when foodstuffs were taxed at a reasonable price. There is no mention of religion made among any of them, except in Cornwall and Norfolk.

SOURCE D

One of the Commonwealth writers attacks landlords for their behaviour. From Robert Crowley, The Way to Wealth, *1550.*

Contrary to the law against oppression and extortion, you have enclosed from the poor their common land, levied greater entry fees payable on new leases, excluded them from their rightful use of the common land, and raised their rents. What obedience did you show when the king's proclamations were sent forth to open up your enclosures, and yet you continued to enclose? If you had loved your country, would you not have prevented the recent great destruction which followed from your incurable greed?

Essay planning

Plan a mini-essay on this topic: 'How serious were the economic problems in the period 1547–50?'

Find four pieces of evidence from this book and your own reading to show that they were serious and explain them and four pieces of evidence to show they were not serious. Write a conclusion based on these points.

The rebellions of 1549

The late spring and summer of 1549 witnessed much of central and southern England facing riot and rebellion, with at least some 25 counties affected. Most rebellions were put down by local gentry, but two – the Western and Kett's – required the use of government troops. Most of the unrest had long-term economic and social factors at the root of the problem, most notably enclosure and rising prices.

The Western rebellion

This has usually been called the Prayer Book rebellion, suggesting it was religiously motivated. Events beforehand suggest there was religious tension as William Body was murdered at Helston in 1548 when he returned to supervise the destruction of images. A large number gathered at Bodmin to protest about the Act of Uniformity, but the major unrest started at Sampford Courtenay on Whitsunday 1549, where locals protested about the new Prayer Book and insisted the priest used the old one. Protest soon spread and rebels from Devon and Cornwall met at Crediton. The rebel demands were largely religious, but this was because they were probably drawn up by priests. They wanted to restore traditional doctrine and asserted a belief in **transubstantiation** and **purgatory**. However, it appears that initial complaints included an attack on the sheep and cloth tax, while the action of the rebels suggests that they disliked the local gentry:

- Gentry were attacked and robbed at St Michael's Mount.
- At Bodmin they shouted 'Kill the gentlemen'.
- They murdered William Hellyons, a local member of the gentry.
- They attacked Trematon Castle.

The rebels laid siege to Exeter, where fears that the city would be handed over to the rebels led the mayor to provide poor relief, firewood and food for the poor.

The dislike of the rebels for the gentry meant that when rebellion broke out they were unable to restrain the commons and the government had to send a force under Lord John Russell. They were slow to deal with the unrest as they had to put down unrest in Oxfordshire and Buckinghamshire en route. However, when they did arrive in the West Country, a number of skirmishes occurred at Fenny Bridges, Clyst St Mary and Clyst Heath, before the rebels were finally defeated at Sampford Courtenay, where some 3000 rebels were killed and further retribution followed.

Kett's rebellion

The rebellion took place in East Anglia and took its name from its leader, Robert Kett. The unrest began as enclosure riots in the towns of Attleborough and Wymondham. The rioters were angry that a local lawyer, John Flowerdew, had bought the local abbey church and begun to enclose the land. He attempted to turn the rebels against Kett, who had also enclosed land, but he turned the rebels against Flowerdew. Kett quickly raised 16,000 men who marched to Norwich and set up a camp on Mousehold Heath. The rebels were offered a pardon, but this failed to disperse them. Instead they seized Norwich. The government sent a force under the Marquis of Northampton, but it was defeated and therefore the Duke of Northumberland was sent. His force massacred the rebels at Dussindale outside Norwich, killing some 3000. Kett was hanged for treason but many rebels were treated leniently.

The rebel demands

These can be put under four headings:

1 Agricultural demands: concern about enclosure, particularly of saffron grounds, gentry abuse of the **foldcourse system** and their overstocking of common land.
2 Economic concerns: rising rents.
3 Social grievances: the gentry's manipulation of local government.
4 Religious concerns: they wanted better preachers and further reform.

Other unrest in 1549

Evidence suggests it was caused by long-term economic changes, but also religion. There was opposition to enclosure, with rebels attacking hedges, but in Oxfordshire, Yorkshire and Hampshire it appears the religious changes were the main cause.

Doing reliability well a

Below are an exam-style question, a set of definitions listing common reasons why sources can be unreliable and Sources A–D. For each source write a critical account of whether it is a reliable or unreliable piece of evidence, justifying your answer by referring to the definitions below.

Using these sources in their historical context, assess the view that religion was the main cause of unrest in 1549.

- **Vested interest**: the source is written so that the writer can protect their own power or interests.
- **Second-hand report**: the writer is not in a position to know and is relying on someone else's information.
- **Expertise**: the source is written on a subject that the author is an expert in.
- **Political bias**: the source is written by a politician and it reflects their political views.
- **Reputation**: the source is written to protect the writer's reputation.

SOURCE A

On behalf of the king, the Archbishop of Canterbury replies to the demands of the Western rebels.

When I first read your request, ignorant men of Devon and Cornwall, I thought that you were deceived by some crafty papist, who devised those articles for you, to request things which you did not understand. The devisers of your articles are extreme papists, wilful traitors, enemies to God, our sovereign and the whole realm. You ask for general councils and holy decrees to be restored, but these are made only for the advancement, glory and greed of the Bishop of Rome.

SOURCE B

Kett and other rebel leaders in Norfolk present their demands to the Privy Council.

That new acts of enclosure be not hurtful to such as hath enclosed saffron grounds.

That no lord of a manor shall use the common land.

That meadow ground may be sold at such a price as it was in the first year of Henry VII's reign.

That priests should be resident in their parishes so that parishioners may be instructed in the laws of God.

SOURCE C

The Venetian ambassador in England reports on the unrest.

There is news of major risings against the government in England, and that the king has retreated to a strong castle outside London. The cause of this is the common land, as the great landowners occupy the pastures of the poor people. The rebels also require the return of the mass, together with the religion as it stood on the death of Henry VIII.

SOURCE D

Protector Somerset writes to a close advisor expressing his views of the rebels.

Some rebels wish to pull down enclosures and parks; some want to recover their common land; others pretend religion is their motive. A number would want to rule for a time, and do as gentlemen have done, and indeed all have a great hatred of gentlemen and regard them as their enemies. The ruffians among them, and the soldiers, who are the leaders, look for loot. So the rebellions are nothing other than a plague and fury among the vilest and worst sort of men.

The Lady Jane Grey affair, 1553

The background to the plot was discussed earlier (page 36). This section will consider whether the challenge was due to religion or politics, although contemporaries probably did not draw a distinction.

Causes of the plot

Historians have debated whether the main factor behind the plot was political or religious.

Political issues

When Northumberland's son married Lady Jane Grey in May 1553 the health of Edward was such that it was believed he would live for a long time. This suggests that Northumberland had not been plotting to further his political career. Northumberland therefore had little to gain politically from it. It was Edward's declining health that changed the situation. The change made to the **Devise** (see page 12) meant that Northumberland became the father-in-law of the prospective queen.

Religious issues

Instead, religious issues should be considered. Edward was a strong Protestant and was concerned about his Catholic half-sister, Mary, taking the throne.

However, once Northumberland's situation changed he did attempt to secure his position, aware that his Protestant beliefs meant he was likely to be excluded by Mary. Northumberland may also have thought that he would gain support from the elite as he had restored stability after the failings of Somerset's rule and many would want that to continue. It could also be argued that those who had gained land from the Dissolution of the Monasteries might support him as they could lose those lands if there was a Catholic restoration.

The threat to Mary

Northumberland was able to have Lady Jane Grey proclaimed queen and, if he had been able to capture Mary before she fled to East Anglia, the plot might have succeeded. Northumberland initially had the support of the Privy Council, but Mary, by raising a force, proclaiming herself queen, issuing proclamations, letters of summons and asking Charles V for help, raised the possibility of civil war.

Northumberland lost his advantage and was forced to leave London to confront Mary and this allowed members of the Privy Council the chance to reconsider their views. Many changed their opinion and gave their support to Mary, while Northumberland failed to gain support as he marched east, with some of his own force deserting. This forced him to abandon his march, retreat to Cambridge and proclaim Mary queen.

Aftermath

The sudden collapse of the plot suggests that it stood no chance. This appears to be reinforced by the enthusiasm with which Mary was greeted when she entered London. Some may have feared a return to instability and therefore supported the legitimate ruler. However, it did place many who had initially supported Northumberland in a difficult position. Nevertheless, the leniency shown to many suggests that Mary considered her position weak and that she needed support:

- She soon released **Gardiner** and Norfolk from jail.
- She appointed **Paget** to the Privy Council.

However, Northumberland, Lady Jane Grey and Guildford Dudley were arrested. Northumberland was soon executed, with the others following later.

Explain the differences by using provenance

1 What does Source A show about Mary's view of her claim?
2 Why and to whom was the letter sent?
3 Where was Mary when the letter was sent and what position was she in?
4 What does Source B show about Mary's claim to the throne?
5 Why was the letter produced and to whom was it addressed?
6 What was happening in London when it was written?

SOURCE A

After the announcement of Lady Jane Grey's accession, Mary writes to the Privy Council, 9 July 1553, sending copies of the letter to many large towns.

It seems strange that you did not tell us of our brother's death on Thursday night. Yet, I rely on your loyalty, considering my status, the good of the country and all your honours. Nevertheless, we know you have assembled a force and naturally we fear some evil. But we can take these actions in gracious part, being ready to fully pardon you to avoid bloodshed and vengeance. We trust not to have to use the service of other true subjects and friends abroad whose rightful cause God shall support. We require you to proclaim our right and title to the crown and government of this realm.

SOURCE B

The Privy Council rejects Mary's claim to the throne, 9 July 1553.

We advise you that our Sovereign Lady Queen Jane is possessed of the crown, not only by good order of old ancient records of this realm, but also by the late King Edward's letters signed with his own hand and sealed with the Great Seal of England, with nobles, councillors and judges agreeing to these letters. We must remind you that owing to the divorce between King Henry VIII and your mother, in accordance with the law of God and confirmed by Acts of Parliament [1534 and 1537], you are illegitimate and unable to inherit the crown.

Using your own knowledge

Which of these statements could be used to assess how reliable Source A is as evidence for Mary's view on her claim to the throne? Indicate by ticking the boxes in the table below.

Statement	Useful	Not useful
Edward's death was kept quiet for two days		
Prominent men in London had been forced to sign the Devise		
Mary Tudor had fled to East Anglia, where she raised forces		
The Council ordered sheriffs and justices near to London to raise forces		
Mary proclaimed herself queen the next day, issued letters of summons and asked for support from Charles V		

Wyatt's rebellion, 1554

Historians are divided over the causes of Wyatt's rebellion, with some emphasising its religious nature, while others stress that it was political and caused by Mary's decision to marry Philip of Spain.

Causes of the rebellion

The timing of the rising suggests that Mary's marriage was the main cause, as no sooner were there rumours of the match than opposition began to develop. Hatred of foreigners was easily aroused and stories soon circulated that the English court would be dominated by Spaniards. There were fears that Mary would be ruled over by her husband and England would be dragged into Habsburg conflicts that did not benefit England. There were soon rumours that Mary was to be removed and replaced by her half-sister Elizabeth and by December 1553 this had turned into a plot. Wyatt's propaganda certainly stressed the issue of marriage, probably aware that it would win him greater support than religious arguments. However, his claims should be seen as propaganda as there is some evidence of religious motivation:

- The leaders of the four-pronged attack had Protestant sympathies.
- The area around Maidstone where he gained most support was Protestant.
- Wyatt received advice from the **deprived** Protestant Bishop of Winchester.
- No prominent member of the plot was Catholic.
- On reaching London, the rebels attacked the property of the newly restored Catholic Bishop of Winchester.

However, at the time of the plot, persecution of Protestants had not started. Economic factors may have helped Wyatt win support as the Kent cloth industry was in decline.

Events

The court was aware of the plot and examined Edward Courtenay, who the plotters were going to marry to Elizabeth. He revealed most of the details and forced the rebels to act before they were fully prepared. Instead of a four-pronged attack, it was only in Kent that rebellion occurred, led by a member of the Kentish gentry, Thomas Wyatt. He had been a loyal supporter of the Tudors and supported Mary against Lady Jane Grey. He was fearful he would lose his position and influence with the arrival of large numbers of foreigners.

The appeal to **xenophobia** made it difficult for the regime to raise forces against Wyatt and he was able to play on the fear of what would happen when Philip arrived in England. Wyatt was able to gather a force of some 3000 men, but instead of marching straight to London, he laid siege to Cooling Castle, near Rochester. This gave Mary time to rally her forces, and with a rallying speech at Guildhall bring the rebellion to an end. However, it had been a threat to Mary:

- Troops sent to deal with Wyatt had changed sides, crying 'We are all Englishmen'.
- Many waited to see what would happen and did not initially support Mary.
- The rising had been close to London.

Aftermath

The lack of punishment that followed the revolt suggests Mary feared that further punishment would provoke more unrest and may explain why both Elizabeth and Courtenay would escape with their lives. It may have been Mary's speech at Guildhall which flattered her supporters and saved her as she ignored the Council's advice to leave London, in the same way that her actions in proclaiming herself queen in 1553 had won her the throne.

The failure of this rebellion, and others in the period, may have caused a change in outlook and made most realise that rebellion was futile, and therefore indirectly strengthened the regime.

! The reliability of a source

Below are an exam-style question, a set of definitions listing common reasons why sources can be unreliable and Sources A–C. For each source, write a critical account of whether it is a reliable or unreliable piece of evidence, justifying your answer by referring to the definitions below.

Using these sources in their historical context, assess the view that Wyatt's rebellion was a serious threat to Mary Tudor.

- **Vested interest**: the source is written so that the writer can protect their own power or interests.
- **Second-hand report**: the writer is not in a position to know and is relying on someone else's information.
- **Expertise**: the source is written on a subject that the author is an expert in.
- **Political bias**: the source is written by a politician and it reflects their political views.
- **Reputation**: the source is written to protect the writer's reputation.

SOURCE A

The imperial ambassador reports to the Emperor Charles V on the situation in England at the start of Wyatt's rebellion.

Wyatt's men have rebelled in Kent, proclaiming that they will not consent to a foreign marriage and that every good Englishman ought to help them fight the Spaniards. Although the rebels use the foreign marriage as an excuse, like Carew, their real causes are religion and to favour Elizabeth. It is said that the rebellion is spreading. We hear news that the French and Scots are hastily fitting out ships and raising troops to aid the rebels. We hear the King of Denmark is joining in, hoping to marry Elizabeth to his son or brother.

SOURCE B

The queen addresses the people of London outside Guildhall as the rebels approach the city on 1 February 1554.

I come personally to tell you how traitorously and rebelliously a number of Kentish men have assembled against their sovereign and her subjects. They first pretended they opposed my marriage, but the Council have spoken to them again and it seems the marriage is merely a Spanish cloak to conceal their real purpose against our religion. My loving subjects, I am your queen with the same royal rights as my father. You were always faithful and loving to him and therefore I do not doubt that you will be as faithful to me. I, being your lady and mistress, tenderly love and favour you in return.

SOURCE C

A well-informed contemporary outlines the major events of the rebellion. From Charles Wriothesley's Chronicle of England *for 1554.*

On 29 January the Duke of Norfolk tried to attack Rochester Castle, where the traitor Wyatt and his rebels lay, but he was forced to flee and the rebels captured his artillery. On 1 February Queen Mary went to the city of London, and denounced Wyatt's attempt to take her crown and sack the city. On 3 February Wyatt's army reached London Bridge. On 7 February the Earl of Pembroke gathered the royal army near at Charing Cross near the city, but Wyatt and some rebels avoided them and got close to the city, where they were captured.

Exam focus (A-level)

Below is a model answer in response to an exam-style A-level question and source. Read the answer and the comments around it.

Using these four sources in their historical context, assess how far they support the view that religious changes were the main cause of unrest in 1549.

SOURCE A

The king, Edward VI, in a letter written for him by Protector Somerset in July 1549, lists some of the demands of the rebels of Devon and Cornwall.

For baptism, you are fearful that your children should now only be christened on holy days. You say certain Cornishmen are offended because they do not have their service in Cornish, since they understand no English.

You object that religious changes were made without my knowledge. But I deny this and affirm that the Prayer Book is according to scripture and the word of God.

You require the tax granted to me by parliament on cloth and sheep be cancelled. You complain of the shortage of food and other things.

SOURCE B

From the demands of Kett's rebels in the summer of 1549.

Article 3: We pray your grace that no lord of the manor encloses the common land.

Article 5: We pray that reed ground and meadow ground are the same rent as they were in the first year of King Henry VII.

Article 8: We pray that priests or vicars that are unable to preach and set forth the word of God to their parishioners may be removed from their benefice and the parishioners choose another.

Article 10: We pray no man under the status of knight or esquire keep a dovecote, unless it has been the custom.

SOURCE C

The Venetian ambassador in England reports on the unrest in 1549 and the government's response.

There is news of major risings against the government in England, and that the king has retreated to a strong castle outside London. The cause of this is the common land, as the great landowners occupy the pastures of the poor people. The rebels also require the return of the mass, together with religion as it stood on the death of Henry VIII. The government, wishing to apply a remedy, put upwards of 500 persons to the sword, sparing neither women nor children.

SOURCE D

Protector Somerset expresses his views about the unrest to a close advisor in a letter, 24 August 1549.

Some rebels wish to pull down enclosures and parks; some want to recover their common land; other pretend religion is their motive. A number would want to rule for a time, and do as gentlemen have done, and indeed all have a great hatred of gentlemen and regard them as their enemies. The ruffians among them, and the soldiers, who are the leaders, look for loot. So the rebellions are nothing other than a plague and a fury among the vilest and worst sort of men.

All four sources comment on the role of religion as a cause of unrest. Source A offers the strongest argument that religion was the main cause, while Sources B and C suggest that it was, along with social and economic issues, a cause, but Source D argues that religion was not a motive, but an excuse as 'others pretend religion is their motive'.

Source A has the strongest argument that religion was the main cause. Somerset, writing on behalf of the young king, acknowledges that many of the demands of the Western rebels concerned religion, noting in particular their demands on christenings and the language of the new service. This view is valid as most of the final demands drawn up the Western rebels were on religious matters, with attacks on the new Prayer Book, which they described as a 'Christmas game', and complaints about the abolition of holy water. This view is further reinforced by the timing of the rebellion, which began immediately after the moderately Protestant Prayer Book was introduced at Whitsun 1549. However, even Somerset's response to the rebels acknowledges that religion was not the only cause as he refers to the tax on sheep and cloth as a cause. This issue was absent from the rebels' final demands and raises doubts about how far those demands reflect the actual grievances of the rebels and instead provide evidence that religion was only pretended to be their motive, as suggested in D, because the rising had been hijacked by the clergy. The actions of the rebels, with their attacks on the gentry, would further suggest that, despite Somerset's comments in A, which stress the religious nature of the rising, the initial causes also included social and economic grievances, such as enclosure and the proposed sheep tax. Somerset, as Lord Protector, would have wanted to be clear about the actual causes in addressing the rebels, and unlike D when his position had deteriorated because of the scale of unrest, would not have needed to cover up the actual causes.

Sources B and C both acknowledge that religion was a cause of the unrest, but neither suggest it was the main cause. Source D argues that the rebels wanted the return of the mass and the religious situation restored to the position it was at Henry VIII's death, and this is supported by the final demands of the Western rebels. However, the ambassador's report does not distinguish between the different rebellions and their causes but writes more generally as he also comments that some rebellions were due to enclosure, which was certainly true of the unrest in East Anglia where the rising began with enclosures being pulled down. His understanding of the causes is therefore supported by the rebel demands and, as he is reporting to the Senate in Venice as ambassador, his role would be to report the actual events. Source B also suggests that religion was a cause of the unrest, but, as the source suggests, religious demands did not dominate. As the source is the demands of the rebels it is likely to reflect their demands and the concern about the loss of common land was genuine in East Anglia as a number of gentry had put large flocks of sheep on common land on which many peasants depended for grazing their own sheep. It is also not surprising that they complained about rents as prices were rising quickly in this period and many were unable to afford the rises, while the final complaint about the gentry and their behaviour is reflected in other demands about rabbit warrens and both their behaviour in local government and the attacks made on them during the rising and at Mousehold Heath, where some were put on trial. Source B does suggest there were religious concerns, but unlike A, the demands were for greater reform and this is further supported by their actions at Mousehold as they brought in Protestant preachers. Both Sources B and C therefore appear to be valid in their interpretation of the causes as they are supported by rebel demands and also their actions.

Source D plays down the role of religion, and although written again by Somerset is in contrast to Source A. However, although Somerset is correct to stress the social and economic causes of unrest, with attacks on enclosures and the gentry seen in much of the country, he is wrong to dismiss religion as it played a role in the West Country, Yorkshire

---

The response establishes an overview of the sources in relation to the question. Such a start suggests that the response will be source driven and that the candidate has a clear understanding of each source about the issue in the question.

Own knowledge is directly linked to the source to explain why the view it offers can be seen to be valid.

Further knowledge is applied, but there is a balanced discussion about the limits to the value of the rebels' demands.

The provenance is considered and a good link is made to D and an explanation offered as to why Somerset's view appears to have changed.

The response deals with B and C together as they both suggest that religion was a cause, if not the main or only cause.

Both sources are evaluated using both their provenance and own knowledge to reach a judgement about them in relation to the question.

and Oxfordshire. His playing down of its role is because his position of Lord Protector was under attack and he was blamed by many of the ruling class for encouraging unrest by his policies, including religion. By the end of August, with his position weakening, having had to call on Northumberland and Russell to suppress the risings in East Anglia and the west, as well as abandon his policy in Scotland, he was trying to bolster his own position and therefore suggested that the religious change was not a genuine cause of unrest, but instead was exploited by Catholic priests to cause disquiet. Although there may be some validity in this view, as seen in the changing nature of the demands of the Western rebels, Somerset's view is coloured by his attempt to preserve his own position and deflect criticism, as he had accepted that religion was an issue in Source A.

> Once again detailed own knowledge and provenance are used to evaluate the source.

The sources do support the view that religion was a cause of unrest, but only A suggests that it was the main cause. The other sources suggest that social and economic causes were at least as important, if not more, than religion and the scale of social unrest in much of central, eastern and southern England would suggest that view has much validity.

> Although the judgement is brief, it is based on the sources and not own knowledge.

All the sources are evaluated using both own knowledge and their provenance. The own knowledge is directly linked to the sources and the response does not simply provide lots of knowledge about the unrest of 1549, but uses it to support or challenge the views offered in the sources. The issue of provenance might have been developed, but the response avoids the use of 'stock' comments and instead comments on developments that had taken place in England to explain why a particular view, as in D, might be offered. The answer remains focused on the question and addresses the question as to whether religion was the main cause. It therefore addresses all the issue required to reach the higher levels.

Considering the provenance

Rewrite the answer so that the provenance of the sources is considered in more detail but avoids using just stock comments.

Read this source and the question/answer on page 49.

SOURCE

Protector Somerset expresses his views about the unrest to a close advisor, 24 August 1549.

Some rebels wish to pull down enclosures and parks; some want to recover their common land; other pretend religion is their motive. A number would want to rule for a time, and do as gentlemen have done, and indeed all have a great hatred of gentlemen and regard them as their enemies. The ruffians among them, and the soldiers, who are the leaders, look for loot. So the rebellions are nothing other than a plague and a fury among the vilest and worst sort of men.

Exam focus (AS-level)

3 Rebellion and unrest

Below is a model answer in response to an AS exam-style question and source. Read the answer and the comments around it.

> Use your knowledge of unrest in 1549 to assess how useful the source [on page 48] is as evidence for the breakdown of stability.

The source provides useful evidence to suggest that stability had broken down in 1549. It explains that not only had rebels attacked enclosures, but also that the social order was under threat as there was 'a great hatred of gentlemen'. These claims are certainly supported by the actions of rebels in East Anglia, where unrest began with attacks on the enclosures of both John Flowerdew and Robert Kett, but also in other parts of the country, with fences pulled down in Surrey and contemporaries even commenting about attacks on enclosures in the West Country. The rebels in both the Western rebellion and Kett's also showed a distinct dislike for their social superiors, which the source suggests, as in the west they attacked gentry at St Michael's Mount and murdered William Hellyons, while in East Anglia Kett established a rebel camp at Mousehold Heath from which he organised an alternative local government and this dislike of the local gentry was further confirmed by the number of articles in their demands which complained about the role of the gentry in local government. The rebels did regard the 'gentlemen' as their enemies as none of the rebellions saw gentry or nobility on the side of the rebels, suggesting there was breakdown in stability. However, Somerset blames the breakdown purely on social issues and states that religion was not a cause, but instead 'pretend religion is a motive', which is not correct as most of the demands of the Western rebels concerned religion and the changes he had brought in.

Precise own knowledge is directly linked to the source to support the view and suggest therefore that it is useful.

Further detailed knowledge is applied.

The view offered in the source is challenged and the reasons for that are developed in the next paragraph.

The source was written by Somerset and therefore as Protector, writing in a letter to a close advisor, it would be expected that not only would he know what the causes were and how serious the problems were, but that he would be able to express his views in a candid manner. However, despite this, by the end of August 1549 Somerset was fighting for his political future and therefore his explanation of the events will be to justify and attempt to improve his own position and may not reflect the actual situation. Somerset would not admit that religion was a cause because it was his religious policies that had brought about the unrest and with members of the government, gentry and nobility attacking him and his policies it is not surprising that he wanted to blame other issues and suggest that the rebellions were a 'plague and fury among the vilest and worst sort of men'.

There is a balanced discussion of the provenance of the source and a judgement, supported by own knowledge, is reached.

As a result, the source is only partially useful as evidence for the breakdown in stability as it is from the leader of a government which was under severe pressure, had at one point lost control of Norwich and been forced to send troops to put down the unrest. However, it does show how Somerset attempted to explain the breakdown and justify his own position.

An overall judgement about the source is reached, which is not simply asserted but is supported.

The source is thoroughly evaluated in relation to the issue in question, using both own knowledge and provenance, rather than just generally. A judgement about the usefulness is reached, which is supported. The use of precise own knowledge that is directly linked to the source and consideration of the provenance would take the response into the higher levels.

What makes a good answer?

List the characteristics of a good answer to an AS Part (a) question, using the example and examiner comments above and the mark scheme on page 7.

4 Elizabeth and religion

The religious problems facing Elizabeth in 1558

One of **Elizabeth**'s priorities on coming to the throne in November 1558 was to settle the religious issue. There were a number of pressures facing Elizabeth in achieving a settlement, namely:

- the unsettled situation at home
- the European situation
- Elizabeth's own preferences.

The situation at home

Frequent religious changes under Elizabeth's predecessors had left many confused and uncertain about religion. **Mary** had restored Catholicism and **Pole** had tried to introduce some reforms to remove abuses. Although the Marian burnings may have overshadowed these efforts, the quality of Marian bishops meant they were unwilling to compromise and were able to defeat Elizabeth's first proposals for a settlement.

The number of Protestants in England in 1558 was unknown. However, they were joined by the returning Marian exiles, many of whom wanted a radical Protestant settlement having experienced the **Calvinism** of Geneva and Zürich.

The impact of the foreign situation

England was still at war with France in 1558 and had lost their last enclave, Calais. Although she was reluctant to give it up, Elizabeth needed peace with France and it might be easier to achieve this if England was not aggressively Protestant, as France was Catholic.

Spain was vital to English interests as it ruled the Netherlands, a vital trading partner. Given Spanish power and their Catholicism, they could threaten England if Elizabeth introduced a Protestant settlement. However, Philip II needed English support to allow Spanish ships to move through the Channel to the Netherlands. He was also concerned that England did not come under French–Scottish dominance. Therefore, Philip was more likely to protect her.

Scotland further complicated the situation. It was allied to France and, in Mary Queen of Scots, had what many Catholics believed a good claim to the English throne. France was eager to promote Mary as an alternative ruler. However, the success of the Protestant lords in removing the regent in 1559 reduced the Catholic threat.

The foreign situation suggested Elizabeth needed to proceed with caution, but although the major powers, particularly Spain, were Catholic, even Philip was willing to put politics before religion and proposed to Elizabeth to maintain the alliance.

Peace was made with France in April 1559 and, although Calais was lost, it did mean that Elizabeth could proceed with the religious settlement.

Elizabeth's attitude

As the daughter of Anne Boleyn, Elizabeth was the symbol of the break with Rome. Catholics did not accept Henry's marriage to Anne and therefore saw Elizabeth as illegitimate. Elizabeth was thus bound to make a Protestant settlement.

She was educated by **humanists** and continued to use an English Bible under Mary.

However, she was careful to keep her personal beliefs quiet. Despite this, she did:

- leave chapel on Christmas Day 1558 when the **host** was elevated, as it implied worshipping the sacrament, a Catholic belief
- react to monks carrying candles and incense, suggesting further dislike of Catholic practices.

But, although this suggested a Protestant outlook, Elizabeth liked church music, silver crosses on the altar and rich **vestments**. She also disliked long sermons from radical Protestants. However, by retaining some of these Catholic practices, she may have been being politically astute and discouraging a possible Catholic crusade.

Develop the argument

Below is the conclusion to an answer on the following question:

Assess the problems facing Elizabeth in achieving a religious settlement, 1558.

Annotate the paragraph to develop the argument as to which factor was the most important.

There were many religious problems facing Elizabeth in 1558. One of the most important was the unsettled religious situation in England. Catholicism was still strong in England after Mary's reign. Pole had done much to reform the Church and the Marian bishops were of high quality and unwilling to accept change. However, the problem was more difficult because of the number of Protestants returning from exile who were opposed to Catholicism. The European situation was also a problem. Elizabeth faced the possibility of an attack from Catholic powers. France had close links to Scotland and might attempt to put its queen, Mary Stuart, on the throne because she was not only Catholic, but had a strong claim to the throne. Spain might also support a Catholic crusade, but Philip was concerned that England might fall under French influence and could therefore support Elizabeth. Elizabeth herself was a Protestant and was the product of Henry VIII's marriage to Anne Boleyn, which many Catholics did not accept and therefore saw Elizabeth as illegitimate. Elizabeth was thus bound to make a Protestant settlement but faced many challenges in establishing it.

Turning assertion into argument   a

Below are a sample exam question and a series of assertions. Read the question and then add a justification to each of the assertions to turn it into an argument.

How serious a threat to Elizabeth was the foreign situation in 1558?

France was a serious threat to England in 1558 because

_____

Scotland was also an important consideration because

_____

Spain was important to England because

_____

However, Spain needed English support because

_____

Although the major European powers were Catholic, the situation was not a threat to Elizabeth because

_____

The Elizabethan religious settlement

Parliament had passed all religious changes since 1529 and therefore Elizabeth would have to get its approval. Although the House of Commons was likely to support her proposals, there was a strong Catholic party in the Lords who could oppose her. The first proposal was approved by the Commons, but all the bishops opposed the idea of a Royal Supremacy and eighteen peers objected to doctrinal changes.

Elizabeth **prorogued** parliament for Easter. When it met again, two bishops were sent to the Tower for disobedience and her title was changed from 'Supreme Head' to 'Supreme Governor', which appeased Catholics who held that the Pope was head of the Church. This Act now passed both Houses. The Act of Uniformity passed the Commons easily, but passed the Lords by only three votes. It passed only because of the absence of the two bishops and the absence of the Abbot of Westminster. Soon after, all the Marian bishops refused to take the Oath of Supremacy and were deprived of their positions.

The Church settlement

The settlement was made up of two major Acts of Parliament and some additional ones.

The Act of Supremacy

- Elizabeth was made Supreme Governor of the Church.
- All clergy and officials had to take an oath to her as Supreme Governor.
- The **heresy laws** were repealed.
- Communion in both bread and wine was authorised.

The Act of Uniformity

- The 1552 Book of Common Prayer was to be used in all churches.
- All must attend church on Sundays or pay a fine of one shilling.
- The ornaments of the church and dress of the clergy were to be those of 1548, but could be changed later if the queen wished.
- When communion was said the words included the forms from both the 1549 and 1552 Prayer Books.
- The 'Black Rubric' from 1552, which denied the real or bodily presence of Christ at communion, was omitted.

Other Acts

- Taxes paid by the Church were to be paid to Elizabeth.
- The monasteries restored by Mary were dissolved and lands were confirmed as the legal possession of those who had acquired them.
- The **royal injunctions** included the requirement for clergy to wear distinctive dress, music was encouraged, congregations were to bow at the name of Jesus and images did not have to be destroyed.
- Clergy could marry, but their wives had to be approved by the bishop.

The settlement has been described as a 'middle way', but although it did not establish a Catholic Church, it was not an extreme Protestant one.

It did not satisfy many Protestants who had left England during Mary's reign. They wanted a settlement that was more Calvinist and the removal of anything that appeared to be Catholic. They disliked bowing at Jesus' name, kneeling to receive communion, the sign of the cross in baptism and the wearing of vestments. They argued these were not in the Bible, but defenders of the settlement argued they were 'matters indifferent', describing them as **adiaphora**. Some also disliked the structure of the Church, particularly the use of bishops, who they disliked because they were appointed by the queen and not the whole Church. Many of these would continue to oppose the settlement and try to get it changed during the course of Elizabeth's reign.

Quick quizzes at **www.hoddereducation.co.uk/myrevisionnotes**

! Spot the mistake

a

Below are a sample exam question and the first paragraph of an answer. Why is this not likely to lead to a high mark? Once you have identified why, rewrite the paragraph.

'The religious settlement satisfied neither Catholics nor Protestants.' How far do you agree?

The religious settlement satisfied neither Catholics nor Protestants for many reasons. The settlement faced opposition in both Houses of Parliament and passed the Lords only when Elizabeth's title was changed from Supreme Head to Supreme Governor. The Act of Uniformity passed the House of Lords by only three votes. However, there were many attempts to satisfy both Catholics and Protestants as when communion was said the words included both the 1549 and 1552 forms. The Black Rubric was also omitted as it denied the real presence of Christ at communion. The clergy still had to wear distinctive dress and Elizabeth continued to encourage music to be played. Images no longer had to be destroyed and clergy could marry, even though Elizabeth did not approve of married clergy. There were therefore many issues that angered either Catholics or Protestants.

! Simple essay style

Below is a sample essay question. Use your own knowledge, information on the opposite page and information from other sections of the book to produce a plan for the question. Choose four general points, and provide three specific pieces of information to support each general point. Once you have planned your essay, write the introduction and conclusion for the essay. The introduction should list the points to be discussed in the essay. The conclusion should summarise the key points and justify your argument.

To what extent was the religious settlement 'a middle way'?

Introduction:
_____
_____

Point 1:
_____

Point 2:
_____

Point 3:
_____

Point 4:
_____

Conclusion:
_____
_____

The Puritan challenge

There is no agreed definition as to what constitutes a Puritan, but all wanted to change the religious settlement, through the House of Commons, propaganda or protests. Initially they gained their name as result of protests in the 1560s about the vestments clergy had to wear. By the 1570s many were protesting about the some of the practices in the Prayer Book and as the period progressed some, although a minority, wanted to establish a separate Church.

The Puritan challenge over vestments

This started in 1565 when Thomas Sampson, Dean of Christ Church Oxford, refused to wear a **surplice** and was **deprived**. The Puritans did win some concessions on this, but still some refused to conform and 37 London preachers were deprived in 1566. However, this was a small number and their appeal for support to Henry Bullinger, a leading reformist in Switzerland, also failed to gain support. Some of those deprived did, however, establish independent churches.

The Puritans in the House of Commons

- The Puritans won a concession over accepting the Thirty-Nine Articles that defined the Church's beliefs. Clergy had to accept only those about doctrine.
- In 1571 the MP Walter Strickland proposed changes to the Prayer Book, but he was summoned before the Privy Council for infringing **royal prerogative** and barred from the House, but later returned. The bill did not appear again.
- Anthony Cope proposed a 'bill and book' to overturn the government of the Church. His proposals would have ended the authority of bishops. Elizabeth sent Cope and four others to the Tower. The government also launched an attack in the Commons against the bill.

This failure led Puritan MPs to change their tactics.

The Puritans and their popular appeal

- Thomas Cartwright, a Cambridge professor, was the leading academic to attack the settlement and particularly the office of bishops. He had his academic freedom of speech removed and his professorship.
- In 1572 the ministers, John Field and Thomas Wilcox, published 'The Admonition to Parliament'. It called for the Church hierarchy to be replaced. Field and Wilcox were arrested and sent to jail. However, it led to their ideas being debated.

The Separatists

Separatists were Puritans who wanted to establish their own Church. The most famous were the Brownists in Norwich. Another group under Henry Barrow and John Greenwood was established in London, but as a result of legislation against **sectaries** they were arrested and executed.

This ended a movement that had attracted only small numbers and was heavily divided. Most Puritans accepted the Church as they could believe what they wanted as long as they attended church on Sunday.

The survival of Puritanism

Despite these setbacks Puritanism did survive. Some Puritan preachers went abroad, but others were protected by Privy Councillors, such as Cecil and Leicester. However, the main reason it survived was due to prophesyings, where clergy came together to discuss the Bible, and through the **classis movement**, where they met to discuss common interests. Nobles and gentry also helped by establishing lectureships and increasing the amount of preaching. This all concerned Elizabeth as it was outside government control.

However, there were limits to its success. Puritans did not have an agreed doctrine; it was Bible-centred and therefore needed people to be literate. But perhaps the most important reason for its limits was the determination of Archbishop Whitgift to enforce conformity. He introduced the Three Articles to which all clergy had to subscribe, or could be suspended. The Puritans also damaged their own cause by the publication of the Marprelate Tracts, which attacked bishops. It shocked many and allowed a clampdown on printing presses. The attack did much to discredit the Puritan cause and many leaders lost the will to fight on.

! Support or challenge?

a

Below is a sample exam question which asks whether you agree with a specific statement. Use your own knowledge and the information on the opposite page to decide whether the sources support or challenge the statement in the question and tick the appropriate box.

'Puritanism was never a serious threat to Elizabeth.' How far do you agree?

	Support	Challenge
The Puritans were able to win some concessions over vestments		
The clergy had to accept only those articles of the Thirty-Nine Articles that concerned doctrine		
Strickland and Cope's proposals to change the Prayer Book and Church government were both defeated		
The Admonition led to its authors being jailed, although the ideas were debated		
Separatists were small in numbers		
Prophesyings could not be controlled by the government		
Archbishop Whitgift enforced conformity using the Three Articles		
The Marprelate Tracts shocked many and lost Puritanism support		

i Introducing an argument

Below are a sample exam question and an introduction. Rewrite the introduction in order to set out an argument that looks at more than one point of view.

How successful was Elizabeth's policy towards Puritanism?

Elizabeth I was very successful in dealing with Puritanism because she was able to prevent changes to the religious settlement of 1558 that Puritans wanted. She was also able to ensure that attempts in the House of Commons to change the Prayer Book and the structure of the Church failed. Those Puritans, such as Field and Wilcox, who also challenged her policies were jailed. Meanwhile the number of Puritans who left the established Church and became separatists were very small and Elizabeth's position was further strengthened by the actions of Archbishop Whitgift who supported the queen in enforcing conformity. The weak position of the Puritans was made worse by their own actions in publishing the Marprelate Tracts, as the scurrilous nature of their attacks justified a further clampdown by the government and caused many Puritans to abandon the cause.

Elizabeth's archbishops and their support

Elizabeth had three Archbishops of Canterbury during her 45-year reign. They were:
- Matthew Parker, 1559–75
- Edmund Grindal, 1575–83
- John Whitgift, 1583–1604.

Matthew Parker

Parker's career began in 1527 and therefore had started before the Reformation. He attended Cambridge University and he had been chaplain to Anne Boleyn. During Mary's reign, although deprived, he remained in England and therefore had not experienced the ideas of Geneva. For these reasons he appealed to Elizabeth. His achievements included the following:
- The passage of the Thirty-Nine Articles, resisting calls for them to be more Protestant.
- Reaching a compromise over vestments and issuing his Advertisements, which told the clergy to accept some uniformity. His compromise initially disappointed Elizabeth, but it also helped to maintain her popularity.
- He provided the settlement with a firm basis.

Edmund Grindal

Like Parker, Grindal was educated at Cambridge. However, during Mary's reign he went into exile. With the resignations of Mary's bishops, Elizabeth was forced to appoint exiles as bishops and he became Bishop of London, then Archbishop of York, followed by Canterbury. He did not want this role and disagreed with Elizabeth over prophesyings, which he thought could be used to improve clerical standards and preaching. Elizabeth disagreed as she disliked preaching and the lack of control the government had over these events. In 1576 he refused to suppress them or send out orders for them to end. Elizabeth was unwilling to accept disobedience and Grindal was punished. He was confined to his house and suspended for six months. Finally he agreed to resign, but died before the process was complete. His suspension meant that for much of his period in office the Church lacked leadership, bringing discredit on it.

John Whitgift

As with Elizabeth's other archbishops, Whitgift was educated at Cambridge. He stayed in England during Mary's reign. He was a distinguished academic, appointed Lady Margaret Professor of Divinity at Cambridge. In 1570 he was appointed Vice-Chancellor of the University. When Cartwright attacked the Church, it was Whitgift who ensured he lost his professorship. In 1572 he replied to the Admonition (see page 54) and was made Bishop of Worcester. In 1583 he became Archbishop of Canterbury. During his time in office he did much to strengthen the Church:
- He used the new **Court of High Commission** to ensure uniformity.
- He introduced the Three Articles.
- He used the **ex-officio oath** so those questioned had to swear to answer the questions truthfully before they knew the questions.
- He and Bancroft, the Bishop of London, clamped down on those responsible for the Marprelate Tracts.

Elizabeth supported Whitgift in his actions, and this was made clear by his appointment as a Privy Councillor.

! Delete as applicable

a

Below are a sample question and a paragraph written in answer to this question. Read the paragraph and decide which of the possible options (in bold) is most appropriate. Delete the least appropriate options and complete the paragraph by justifying your selection.

'Elizabeth received considerable support from her archbishops.' How far do you agree?

> Elizabeth's archbishops were **very/mostly/quite/not very** supportive of her. The archbishops supported her to a **limited/fair/great** extent in upholding the settlement of 1558–59. Matthew Parker was able to ensure that **all/most/some/a few** Puritans accepted the changes Elizabeth had introduced. Edmund Grindal was **more/less** willing to support Elizabeth against the **Catholics/Puritans** and this meant that his relationship with the queen was **strong/poor** as he **agreed/disagreed** with her attitude towards prophesyings. However, it was under John Whitgift that the queen received **the greatest/some/least** support. He was particularly **successful/unsuccessful** in strengthening the Church. He was determined to enforce conformity and to a **limited/fair/great** extent this was achieved and he had **great/limited/some** success in destroying Puritanism as a threat to the Church.

⚕ Identify an argument

a

Below are a series of definitions, a sample exam question and two sample conclusions. One of the conclusions achieves a high level because it contains an argument. The other achieves a lower level because it contains only assertion. Identify which is which.

- **Description**: a detailed account.
- **Assertion**: a statement of fact or an opinion, which is not supported by a reason.
- **Reason**: a statement that explains or justifies something.
- **Argument**: an assertion justified with a reason.

How effective were Elizabeth's archbishops at enforcing religious conformity?

Sample 1

> Matthew Parker and John Whitgift were all effective to some extent, but Edmund Grindal was not effective. Parker, as her first archbishop, ensured that the religious settlement was established and Whitgift took action to undermine or remove those who challenged it, but Grindal did not, in fact he would not suppress opponents. Grindal therefore did much to discredit the Church and was not effective, but Whitgift's actions did much to restore Church authority.

Sample 2

> Matthew Parker and John Whitgift were more effective at enforcing religious conformity than Edmund Grindal. Grindal's refusal to take action against prophesyings and his subsequent suspension meant that the Church lacked effective leadership for part of the period and prevented conformity from being enforced. However, both Parker and Whitgift ensured that there was conformity, Parker through actions such as compromising over vestments with some Puritan clergy, while Whitgift took a firm line, using the Court of High Commission to enforce conformity, but also clamping down on those who published the Marprelate Tracts and discrediting more extreme Puritanism. Therefore, for much of the period Elizabeth's archbishops were effective in enforcing conformity and, even after Grindal's tenure, the Church was able to recover.

The Catholic challenge

In the early years of Elizabeth's reign, the Roman Catholic threat was limited. Despite initial fears, there was little evidence of foreign support for a crusade. At home, many Catholics simply attended services, but maintained their inward beliefs. There were few who refused to go to church. However, the situation changed in 1568 when Mary Stuart, or Queen of Scots, arrived in England.

The challenge from Mary Queen of Scots

Forced to **abdicate** the Scottish throne and imprisoned, she escaped and came to England. Mary was both an **anointed** queen and had a claim to the English throne. If Elizabeth sent her back she might be killed, or if she regained power might attack England. In England she could build up support and challenge Elizabeth's position.

The Northern Earls Rebellion, 1569–70

Elizabeth's concerns about Mary became clear within a year of her arrival as the Catholic earls Northumberland and Westmorland led a rising. Mass was briefly restored in Durham Cathedral and Mary's claim to the throne was put forward. The rebellion was defeated and Mary was moved further south, but it showed that she had the potential to be a threat.

Papal excommunication

In 1570 the Pope, Pius V, issued the **papal bull**, *Regnans in Excelsis*, which excommunicated and deposed Elizabeth. Catholics were now absolved from recognising Elizabeth as queen.

Catholic plots

- In 1571 Roberto Ridolfi plotted with the Spanish ambassador to marry Mary to the Duke of Norfolk and put her on the throne.
- In 1583 Francis Throckmorton plotted with the Spanish ambassador to kill Elizabeth.
- In 1586 Anthony Babington plotted to kill Elizabeth and make England Catholic using Spanish troops.

The plots and events in Europe, such as the **St Bartholomew's Day Massacre** and the assassination of William of Orange, convinced many that Protestantism was under threat and this led to a series of measures:

- In 1584 parliament set up a Bond of Association under which anyone linked to plots against Elizabeth could be executed.
- In 1586 England signed the Treaty of Berwick with Scotland and promised James VI a pension as long as Scotland remained friendly.

- In 1586 the Privy Council put more pressure on Elizabeth to execute Mary, which finally happened in 1587.

Catholicism had become a threat because of its international links with European monarchs and the papacy. Catholics within England either did not want to, or were not strong enough, to overthrow Elizabeth.

The arrival of seminary priests and the Jesuits

Elizabeth hoped that Catholicism would die out naturally, but this did not happen because of the determination of William Allen. He established a seminary at Douai to train priests to go to England. They would be able to give the sacraments and administer rites, thus keeping the faith alive. The first priests arrived in 1574. Their success was evident by the government response as Cuthbert Mayne was executed in 1577 for treason. The Jesuits emerged in the 1580s and in 1581 parliament passed an Act which increased **recusancy fines** to £20 per month and made it treason to recognise the authority of Rome or encourage others. In 1585 it was made treasonable to be an ordained Catholic priest in England.

About 100 seminary priests came before 1580 and, after 1580, 179 came in a five-year period, 24 of whom were executed. In total some 650 Jesuits and seminary priests came and 133 were executed as traitors, with numbers peaking around 1588. Their achievements are a matter of controversy among historians, with some arguing they confined their work to the south-east and to providing for gentry households. Others have argued that through the gentry households they kept the faith alive.

The problems facing Catholics, 1558–89

- Elizabeth's longevity meant Catholicism was dying out.
- Government legislation, fines and treason Acts limited the appeal.
- They lacked effective support from abroad.
- There was a shortage of Catholic priests to keep the faith alive; as they died they were not replaced.
- Some Catholics went abroad.
- The execution of Mary Queen of Scots removed the figurehead.
- The defeat of the Spanish Armada.
- There were social pressures to conform.

! Complete the paragraph

Below are a sample exam question and a paragraph written in answer to the question. The paragraph lacks a clear point at the start, but does contain supporting material and an explanatory link back to the question at the end. Complete the paragraph by writing in the key point at the start in the space provided.

Assess the reason why Elizabeth was more concerned by the Catholic challenge in the period after 1570 than before.

_____

_____

_____

_____

This point is supported by events in France and the Netherlands. The St Bartholomew's Day massacre appeared to provide evidence that there was a European conspiracy to eradicate Protestantism. This was only reinforced by events in the Netherlands, where the Protestant leader, William of Orange, was assassinated and the Dutch rebels were struggling to survive against Spanish forces. The threat of such developments to England was made clear in the measures that the government took to try to ensure the queen's safety and the pressure that was put on her to remove Mary Stuart. These developments can be contrasted with the period before 1570 when the Spanish king, Philip II, supported Elizabeth and had dissuaded the Pope from excommunicating her, which had made her position more secure in the early years.

! Spider diagram

Use the information on the opposite page and your own knowledge to add detail to the spider diagram below to identify how serious the Catholic threats were to Elizabeth.

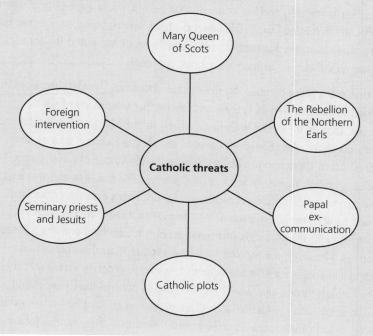

Exam focus

Below is a model answer in response to an exam-style question. Read the answer and the comments around it.

Assess the problems Elizabeth faced in 1558.

When Elizabeth succeeded to the throne in 1558 there were many who did not think that she would survive as monarch, such were the problems she faced. Not only was she viewed as illegitimate in Catholic eyes but both the religious situation at home and the foreign situation made her position weak. She also inherited a substantial debt from Mary and a country that had been ravaged by disease, as well as a series of poor harvests. It was the religious issue that was her greatest problem as it not only divided the country but had an impact on her legitimacy and the foreign situation.

The opening outlines the problems Elizabeth faced and does offer a view as to the seriousness of them.

The religious problem was the most serious problem Elizabeth faced. The country was divided religiously as the religious pendulum had swung backwards and forwards since Henry VIII's break with Rome. Although Edward VI had introduced a large measure of Protestant reform, this had been reversed by Mary. Religious tensions were high and this was made worse by Elizabeth's own religious views which certainly favoured Protestantism. However, the bishops who Mary had appointed were unwilling to accept a reversal of religious direction while Protestant exiles returning from the continent after Mary's death wanted a fully reformed Church similar to that of Calvin's Geneva.

The paragraph explains why religion was the most serious problem facing her.

Elizabeth position was made more difficult because of questions over her legitimacy. She was viewed as illegitimate by many Catholics who did not accept the legality of Henry VIII's marriage to Anne Boleyn and therefore saw the Catholic, Mary Stuart, as the rightful heir. Elizabeth's own religious beliefs also favoured Protestantism; she was the symbol of the break with Rome and had been tutored by humanists or Protestants. During Mary's reign she had continued to use an English Bible, further signifying her beliefs. However, any change to the religious position in England would need parliamentary approval and there was bound to be problems in getting legislation through a Catholic-dominated House of Lords. Therefore, although questions about her legitimacy and her own religious beliefs, made even clearer when she left the Royal Chapel on Christmas Day 1558 when the host was elevated, suggested that a Protestant settlement was essential, the support for Catholicism at home and the foreign situation suggested either a Catholic, or at best a cautious approach.

The question of her legitimacy is linked to the religious issue as the reason why religion is the most serious problem is further developed.

The religious problem is further explained.

The religious situation was made more complex by the foreign situation. The Catholic claimant, Mary Stuart, was married to the Dauphin of France and her mother was Mary of Guise, which gave the French a reason to intervene in England to try to put Mary on the throne. This situation was made worse as when Elizabeth came to the throne England was at war with France as a result of Mary supporting Spain and her husband Philip in the Habsburg–Valois wars. The religious situation therefore made a religious crusade possible and this was made more likely by the peace signed between France and Spain. There was the possibility that Elizabeth could face a joint Franco-Spanish attack to maintain the Catholic religion and this was made more likely by the presence of French troops in Scotland and the alliance between those two nations. However, the problem was less serious than this suggests as it was unlikely that Philip would support a crusade against England in order to install a French-backed monarch on the English throne who would then be able to control the Channel and communications between Spain and the Netherlands. This was soon evident by Philip's offer of marriage to Elizabeth, despite their religious differences. Therefore, although the foreign situation appeared to be a particular problem, Philip's prioritising of strategic concerns over

A further link between religion and another issue is made.

The reason why the foreign situation was a serious problem is explained.

religious lessened the challenge to Elizabeth and this became even more apparent when Philip persuaded the Pope not to excommunicate her, which further reduced the risk of a Catholic crusade.

However, the balance ensures that the answer continues to put forward the view that religion as opposed to the foreign situation is the greater problem.

The lack of foreign support for a religious crusade against Elizabeth helped to make her position more secure as many did not want a return to the instability that had gripped the period from 1549 to 1555. Provided Elizabeth acted cautiously there were many who were willing to accept a moderate settlement, while the lack of papal support meant those who wanted to remove Elizabeth lacked leadership of the resources. However, that did not mean that it would be easy for Elizabeth to bring about religious change through parliament.

The last point is further developed.

The war with France was a further problem for Elizabeth as not only did it threaten security, but it was a drain on resources. Elizabeth inherited a debt of some £227,000 from Mary and most of this was the result of the French war, but this was less of a problem than the religious situation as peace was made with France in April 1559. Moreover, the financial position was also resolved, although only in the long term, through the revised Book of Rates which increased the revenue from custom duties.

The problem of finance is considered and it is clearly explained why this is less of a problem.

At home, Elizabeth also faced the problem of rising prices, poverty, disease and poor harvests. Some 200,000 had probably been killed by a flu epidemic and this created an atmosphere of pessimism and made it difficult to generate the wealth needed for a prosperous economy, which was made worse by continual debasement. This atmosphere was only added to by the loss of Calais in the French wars and the legacy of the Marian burnings. As a result, many were therefore quite pleased to see the end of Mary's reign and welcomed the accession of Elizabeth, providing her with the potential of support if she and her government could provide stability.

Although social and economic issues could be seen as a problem, which in part could not be solved, the response uses them to suggest that they could be used to Elizabeth's advantage.

Elizabeth faced a series of problems, but it was the religious issue that was the greatest challenge. Both domestically and internationally a cautious or even Catholic approach appeared to offer the best solution, but the question of legitimacy in Catholic eyes and her own beliefs made this impossible. The religious divisions and expectations within the country only compounded the problem. The foreign threat was lessened because Philip placed politics before religion, while the financial issue was partially solved by making peace with France, while the social and economic issues were a further complication, but also offered Elizabeth the potential for support if the government appeared to offer stability.

The judgement supports the line of argument pursued throughout the answer.

This is a strong answer that considers a good range of issues and follows a consistent line of argument. Links are made between a range of factors and this helps to take the response into the higher mark band. The argument is well supported; however, the ideas in the last main paragraph could have been developed.

Reaching a judgement

In order to reach the very top level, candidates need to reach judgements about the issues they are considering in relation to the question. Identify paragraphs where the candidate has done this successfully and those where a judgement is either absent or not developed. In the latter case, write a couple of sentences for each of the paragraphs so that a judgement based on the argument is reached.

5 The nature of Elizabethan monarchy, government and parliament

The role of the court, ministers and Privy Council

The court

The royal court existed wherever the queen might be. There were two main areas to the court, the **Presence Chamber**, where the monarch might be seen, and the **Privy Chamber**, to which access was guarded. The ceremonial aspects of court became more important and were used as a means of control. **Elizabeth** turned many of her politicians into courtiers. The court was also used for private rituals, with masques reinforcing the image of **Gloriana**. Being present at court gave courtiers access to the queen and this was vital in influencing decisions and gaining patronage. During the summer the court would embark on royal progresses or tours; although these were confined to the south, home counties and East Anglia, it did give people an opportunity to see their queen and were a major public relations exercise.

The Privy Council and ministers

The Privy Council developed from the group of advisors who accompanied the monarch as she travelled. Elizabeth chose her councillors from a small group, summoning probably no more than a dozen at a time. She did not attend their meetings regularly and did not have to accept their advice, but would rarely completely ignore it. The Council met regularly, daily when there were difficulties, and was therefore in immediate control of events.

There were three main groups of councillors:
1 The nobility who were seen as the monarch's natural advisors.
2 Those with experience from previous monarchs.
3 Those whom Elizabeth considered suitable.

She was willing to use those who had served **Mary** if they had particular expertise. The new appointments were from among those who had been loyal to her. She tried to maintain a balance of opinion. However, by the end of her reign the Council was composed largely of officials and had become smaller.

Many issues were discussed at Council meetings and these included:
- the illness of the queen, with smallpox, in 1562
- the possibility of the queen's marriage to Alençon
- the management of Mary Queen of Scots
- the assassination of William of Orange and aiding the Dutch rebels.

They also discussed more mundane matters such as the condition of roads and food supplies.

The core team in the 1570s was **William Cecil** (Lord Burghley), Leicester and Walsingham. They were joined by Hatton and at times Elizabeth consulted Sussex.

How important was William Cecil?

Cecil's relationship with Elizabeth lasted forty years and ended only with his death in 1598. Even then, he ensured his son, Robert, succeeded him, but the roles of Leicester and Walsingham were also important.

Cecil's role was important as he:
- created an intelligence service
- managed the House of Commons and Lords
- created a propaganda system
- drafted Elizabeth's correspondence with foreign ambassadors
- ensured the Privy Council was efficient
- pursued a prudent economic policy so that when Elizabeth died the debt was small.

His work rate was incredible. He was involved in all the important decisions of Elizabeth's reign, most notably the death of Mary Queen of Scots. He also ensured that finance and administration were effective during the war with Spain.

Spectrum of significance

Below are a sample exam question and a list of general points, which could be used to answer it. Use your knowledge and the information on the page opposite and on page 66 to reach a judgement about the relative importance of the factors. Write numbers on the spectrum below to indicate their relative importance. Having done this, write a brief justification of your placement on the line, explaining why some of these factors are more important than others. The resulting diagram could form the basis of an essay plan.

'The court was the most important element in Elizabethan government.' How far do you agree?

1 The ceremonial aspects of the court were used to maintain control.

2 Presence at court gave access to the queen.

3 The Privy Council met regularly and was in immediate control of events.

4 Issues such as marriage, the succession and Mary Queen of Scots were discussed at Council meetings.

5 The role of parliament.

6 The role of ministers.

Least important ⟵——————————————————————————————⟶ Most important

Eliminate irrelevance a

Below are a sample exam question and a paragraph written in answer to the question. Read the paragraph and identify the parts of the paragraph that are not directly relevant to the question. Draw a line through the information that is irrelevant and justify your deletions in the margin.

How important was William Cecil in the government of England?

Cecil played a very important role in Elizabethan government for much of the period. His role in government ended only with his death in 1598, when he was succeeded by his son Robert, who would also play an important role in the reign of Elizabeth's successor, James I. Although there were other important ministers, such as Leicester and Walsingham, Cecil was involved in all the major decisions made during Elizabeth's reign, most notably the execution of Mary Queen of Scots. Mary was a serious threat to Elizabeth as she had a strong claim to the throne and was seen as the legitimate ruler by some Catholics. It was Cecil who persuaded Elizabeth to sign the death warrant following a series of plots against the queen. He also ensured that during the long conflict with Spain that English finances remained such that the war could be prosecuted. He was also important in the day-to-day administration of the country, writing letters to ambassadors and managing parliament so that Elizabeth's wishes were fulfilled.

Elizabeth, faction and the role of gender

What was faction?

Faction was the result of patronage. A patron would obtain posts for his clients and in return they supported him and therefore built up a faction. Although factions were usually centred on people, such as Cecil or Leicester, they could also develop around causes. Factions had the potential to be dangerous, particularly if the monarch favoured one faction, as happened in 1601 with the Essex rebellion (see page 92). For most of the period Elizabeth used faction to her advantage.

The main factions

- At the start of her reign two main factions emerged under William Cecil and **Robert Dudley**. When it appeared that Elizabeth would marry Dudley, Cecil despaired. The two men differed on policies, with Dudley often wanting to adopt a more aggressive foreign policy. Cecil wanted a more peaceful policy because of the cost and condition of English defences.
- There was a factional clash in 1565–66 between Dudley, now Earl of Leicester, and Thomas Howard. The latter accused Dudley of murdering his wife so he could marry the queen. When a duel appeared possible, Elizabeth announced she would not marry Dudley.

These events suggest Elizabeth was the victim of faction, but she was able to manage it often by not making decisions, which angered both sides.

Factional struggles did result in the execution of two courtiers:
- Norfolk was executed in 1572 after the Ridolfi plot.
- **Essex** was executed in 1601 after his rebellion.

Factional rivalry was made worse because Leicester easily took offence. He also resented the rise of Sir Christopher Hatton and the influence of Thomas Heneage, a gentleman of the Privy Chamber. He was also a rival with Cecil over patronage.

Despite these issues, Elizabeth did control faction as the aim of courtiers was to gain favour. They did not gain her favour by arguing.

The role of gender

Although there was hostility to the idea of a female ruler (see page 10), there were a number of female European rulers at the time. Elizabeth believed that she was divinely ordained to rule.

With her accession, all members of the Privy Chamber, except guards, were women. They were very loyal to her and did not disclose information to courtiers or ambassadors.

There were some difficulties that resulted from her gender. She was jealous at others' happiness and did not congratulate Mary Shelton, a lady of the Privy Chamber, when she married. She threatened to send Leicester to the Tower when he remarried. This type of behaviour could damage the government as it took up time and those out of favour could be exiled.

However, on many occasions she used her gender to her advantage, binding men to her. This was seen in the career of Hatton, who even remained single to please her. She loved flattery and sought praise to enhance her reputation, seen in the dedication of *The Faerie Queen* by Edmund Spenser, in which he equated Fairyland with Elizabethan England, and Gloriana as Elizabeth. She was also portrayed in other works as Judith or Deborah.

She used her ladies of the Privy Chamber to gain information about political gossip.

The queen's Accession Day became a day of celebrations, with jousting and knights showing loyalty to the Virgin Queen.

She exploited her gender in marriage negotiations with Alençon, calling him her 'frog'. She had similar pet names for Leicester and Hatton.

You're the examiner

Below are a sample exam question and a paragraph written in answer to this question. Read the paragraph and the mark scheme provided on page 7. Decide which level you would award the paragraph. Write the level below along with a justification for your decision.

How successfully did Elizabeth I manage factional struggles?

Elizabeth was quite successful at managing factional struggles throughout her reign. It was only in the 1590s, when the Cecil faction were so dominant, that the factional battle resulted in Essex rebelling as he had lost his influence and was unable to reward his supporters. Although there were struggles earlier in the period, Elizabeth was able to exploit them and used them to ensure that she received a range of views which allowed her to reach a balanced decision. Although there were clashes between Cecil and Dudley in the early part of her reign, she was able to resolve the conflict by announcing she would not marry Dudley. She was also willing, when factional tensions caused struggles, to take action. Essex was executed in 1601 and she also executed Norfolk in 1572, following the Ridolfi plot, clear evidence that she and not courtiers were in control. Moreover, she was aware that the aim of factions was to gain influence and she was able to play off the various groups and achieve compromise often by not making decisions, as the factional groups were aware that they would achieve even less by arguing with the queen.

Level:

Reason for choosing that level:

_____

_____

_____

_____

Recommended reading

Below is a list of suggested further reading on this topic.
- *England 1485–1603*, pages 198–202, Mary Dicken and Nicholas Fellows (2015)
- *Elizabeth I*, Christopher Haigh (1988)
- *The Reign of Elizabeth*, pages 58–61, Barbara Mervyn (2001)
- *Elizabeth I and the Government of England*, Keith Randell (1994)

The roles and management of the Lords and Commons

Parliament consisted of the House of Lords and House of Commons. The House of Lords was made up of about 60 nobles and the archbishops and bishops. The Commons consisted of some 400 MPs, although the number grew during Elizabeth's reign; some were elected by **boroughs**, others by the counties. Laws could be proposed by the government or MPs, but needed the approval of both Houses and to receive royal consent to be passed.

Parliamentary meetings

Parliament was not a regular part of the government and was not summoned each year. Sessions were usually limited to a few weeks, often in the spring or autumn. Attendance by MPs was not regular and in 1571 fines were introduced for non-attendance. This suggests that it was MPs who disliked being summoned, particularly because of the cost of staying in London. Elizabeth summoned only 13 parliaments in 45 years, whereas 28 had met in the 30 years before 1558.

The management of parliament

The queen could manage parliament by dissolving it so that fresh elections had to be held or by proroguing parliament, which would mean the same MPs would return when it was called back. Elizabeth also used messages and rumours to direct debates and explain her wishes. If this failed to stop criticism, she possessed the powers of arrest and **veto**. In 1576 Peter Wentworth was sent to the Tower for demanding freedom of speech. Councillors, certainly until the 1590s, ensured that parliamentary business was under their control. They drew up agendas and managed debates. They ensured parliament had less freedom of speech and cut down time for speeches. Elizabeth also influenced the choice of Speaker and this was important as he controlled debates, directed the order of business and could direct the Commons as the queen wanted.

The House of Lords

It used to be thought that the House of Commons was the more important of the two Houses. However, it is unlikely that Elizabeth would have promoted Cecil to the Lords if that was the case. As her parliamentary manager she would have wanted him where there was most business. Certainly once he was in the Lords, business there increased and the Lords was used to put pressure on the Commons through its collective social weight.

Conflict between Elizabeth and parliament

Some historians argued that there was conflict over issues such as:
- religion
- marriage and the succession
- freedom of speech
- **monopolies**.

Religion

There were clashes over religion as Elizabeth was determined the settlement would not be changed. In 1571 Strickland was suspended but this aroused so much opposition it was never done again.

Marriage and the succession

These were major concerns for MPs and the issues were raised in a number of her parliaments (see page 68).

Freedom of speech

Some MPs challenged Elizabeth forbidding the discussion of certain topics. The sending of Wentworth to the Tower by MPs suggests they saw him as a nuisance, not a hero. It does not support the view that the Commons was trying to assert its power.

Monopolies

In 1598 and 1601 Elizabeth needed money for the war against Spain and in Ireland. Some MPs used this an opportunity to complain about the misuse of the **royal prerogative** over monopolies. Elizabeth was forced into cancelling some of them and into making her **Golden Speech** in the 1601 parliament. The Commons also claimed the right to initiate any vote for money and granted the crown only a fraction of its request.

! Complete the paragraph   a

Below are a sample exam question and a paragraph written in answer to the question. The paragraph contains a point and specific examples, but lacks a concluding explanatory link back to the question. Complete the paragraph, adding this link in the space provided.

How effectively did Elizabeth manage her parliaments?

During Elizabeth's reign there were clashes over a number of issues, most notably over religion, freedom of speech and monopolies. A number of MPs were sent to the Tower during her reign, but as in the case of Wentworth this was by the Commons themselves, although Elizabeth did suspend Walter Strickland, which caused disquiet. The clashes over monopolies in the 1590s and in her last parliament of 1601 forced Elizabeth to cancel some of them, but she was able to win back much support by her Golden Speech, which even left some MPs in tears. Elizabeth was also careful to ensure that parliament was managed through her councillors, who ensured that time for debate was reduced and that freedom of speech was restricted. She further enhanced her control by influencing the election of the Speaker who controlled business and could influence MPs. Elizabeth herself also had the power of veto, dissolution and proroguing parliament, which further increased her control.

_____

_____

_____

_____

! Simple essay style

Below is a sample exam question. Use your own knowledge and information on the opposite page and page 62 to produce a plan for the question. Choose four or five general points, and provide three pieces of specific information to support each general point. Once you have planned your essay, write the introduction and conclusion for the essay. The introduction should list the points to be discussed in the essay. The conclusion should summarise the key points and justify which point was the most important.

How important were Elizabethan parliaments in the government of England?

The impact of the marriage and succession and parliamentary privilege

When Elizabeth came to the throne in 1558 it was expected that she would marry. Discussion was about who she would marry, not if she would marry.

Why did Elizabeth need to marry?

- To provide an heir to the throne.
- To preserve the Tudor dynasty.
- The descendants were from the sisters of Henry VIII and nearly all female.
- It was believed a queen needed a king to support and advise her.

The situation was made worse in 1562 when Elizabeth nearly died of smallpox. The situation was eased somewhat by the birth of James VI to Mary Queen of Scots in 1566. Elizabeth tacitly recognised he would be her successor.

Who were Elizabeth's suitors?

- Robert Dudley was a royal favourite. However, the family had a poor reputation. He was already married and the death of his wife, Amy Robsart, in mysterious circumstances, caused rumours to spread that he had murdered her. This would have discredited Elizabeth.
- Philip II would have been unpopular, as Mary's marriage to him had shown. He was a devout Catholic and she could not accept a papal dispensation to allow it as she did not recognise papal authority.
- Archduke Charles, son of the Emperor Ferdinand I, but also a Catholic.
- Prince Eric of Sweden. He sent his brother Duke John of Finland to press his case, but feared John pushed his own candidacy and recalled him.
- Duke of Anjou gained support as relations with Spain deteriorated, but his Catholicism prevented it.
- Duke of Alençon, who was less committed to the Catholic religion, but there was opposition from the public and the Privy Council was divided.

Why was Elizabeth unwilling to marry?

- She had witnessed the disastrous marriages of her father and this may have put her off.
- She realised that it was not a good idea to marry a fellow monarch as Mary Tudor had.
- There was no one suitable.
- She needed a Protestant husband and most suitors were Catholic.
- The English disliked foreigners and wanted a Protestant king.
- She wanted to be in charge and said 'I will have but one mistress and no master'.

The impact of marriage and the succession on domestic affairs

Parliament was concerned that she did marry, presenting a petition as early as 1559. In 1563 they again urged her to marry. She refused to name a successor, as an heir would have been the focus of plots against her. It led to arguments with House of Commons and she forbade discussion of her marriage and succession, but Wentworth demanded freedom of speech (see page 66). She also punished the MP, John Stubbs, for his pamphlet against the French marriage, and had his right hand chopped off.

The impact on foreign affairs

Much of the impact related to Mary Queen of Scots (see page 70) as Elizabeth's potential heir. She was supported by the French Guise family once she had become Queen of France. However, the threat diminished once she returned to Scotland. Mary wanted to be recognised as Elizabeth's heir, but her actions (see page 70) ensured it would be her son who was implicitly recognised as successor.

Spain became more willing to support Mary as relations with England declined and were involved in plots against Elizabeth (see page 70).

Although the issue of succession had the potential to cause problems, its impact was limited.

ⓘ The flaw in the argument

Below are a sample exam question and part of an answer to it. Identify the flaw in the argument and suggest how the answer could be improved. Write your answers below.

'The impact of the succession on domestic issues was very limited.' How far do you agree?

> The question of the succession had a serious impact on Elizabeth's relations with parliament. Parliament was concerned that Elizabeth married in order to produce an heir and secure the succession, particularly as Mary Stuart, a Catholic, had the strongest claim to succeed. This had even led to parliament presenting her with a petition calling on her to marry as early as 1559. The pressure from parliament was ever-present and it led to considerable conflict with the monarch, who forbade its discussion and this caused clashes over the royal prerogative and the issue of freedom of speech. It would therefore be wrong to argue it had very limited impact as there were continuous clashes with the House of Commons.

The flaw is:

_____

The paragraph could be improved by:

_____

_____

ⓘ Turning assertion into argument　a

Below are a sample exam question and a series of assertions. Read the question and then add a justification to each of the assertions to turn it into an argument

'The issue of Elizabeth's marriage caused serious problems.' How far do you agree?

The question of Elizabeth's marital status caused problems in parliament because

_____

_____

However, parliament was unable to achieve anything because

_____

_____

It also created disquiet at court because

_____

_____

However, negotiations over possible marriage improved her position overseas because

_____

_____

The impact of Mary Queen of Scots

In 1559 Mary was Queen of Scotland in her own right and Queen of France, with her husband, Francis II, as king. The French were eager to promote her claim to the English throne. This worried the Spanish who feared the development of a bloc of French-controlled territory and were therefore willing to support Elizabeth. However, in 1560 the death of Francis changed the situation as she was no longer Queen of France. Her mother, Mary of Guise, had also died, and government in Scotland had been taken over by the Protestant Lords of the Congregation. This also led to the Treaty of Edinburgh, which saw French troops removed from Scotland. Mary finally returned to Scotland in 1561, having agreed to recognise the Protestant Church. However, she refused to give up her claim to the English throne.

Mary's arrival in England

In 1568 Mary arrived in England as she had been forced to abdicate and was held prisoner, but she escaped. This increased the threat to Elizabeth because Mary was in England and:
- was an anointed queen
- had a strong claim to the English throne
- had produced a child
- was Catholic.

This placed Elizabeth in a difficult position. If she sent Mary back and she was killed Elizabeth would be blamed. If Mary triumphed in Scotland she would be an even greater threat. She could send Mary to France, but they might help her try to gain the English throne. She could bring Mary to court, but Mary would build up support and be able to make a challenge for the throne. She could keep her in prison, but plots were likely and courtiers were also likely to try to gain Mary's favour in case she became queen. The Northern Earls Rebellion (see page 58), soon after Mary arrived, showed the threat she presented.

Mary's execution

The only way to stop conspiracies and plots was to execute Mary. However, Elizabeth feared how the European powers would respond and whether they would use it as an excuse to launch a Catholic crusade. The factors that forced Elizabeth to execute Mary gradually built up:
- In 1569 the Northern Earls Rebellion put forward Mary as a claimant to the throne. There was a plan to marry her to the Duke of Norfolk, which might also result in a Catholic heir. The Privy Council demanded Norfolk's execution, but Elizabeth refused.
- In 1570 a papal bull (see page 58) excommunicated and deposed Elizabeth. Catholics were now absolved from obeying her and it meant that Mary was seen as their rightful queen, encouraging them to rebel.
- In 1571 the Ridolfi plot proposed to marry Mary to Norfolk and this led the 1572 parliament to urge Elizabeth to execute them both. Norfolk was executed to placate the Commons.
- The 1572 St Bartholomew's Day Massacre convinced many Protestants there was a European conspiracy to wipe out their religion.
- In 1580 the Pope stated that anyone assassinating Elizabeth with the intention of doing God's service would gain merit.
- In 1583 the Throckmorton plot proposed to murder Elizabeth and put Mary on the throne.
- 1n 1584 the Dutch Protestant leader, William of Orange, was assassinated, raising fears that Elizabeth would be next.
- In 1585 Philip II settled his differences with French Catholics and promised to help Mary.
- In 1586 Babington plotted to kill Elizabeth and put Mary on the throne.

The actions of Mary and her supporters, the situation in Europe and the strong feeling among both the Council and parliament made it difficult for Elizabeth to resist their demands that she sign Mary's death warrant. Although Walsingham's spy network had prevented the plots from succeeding, there was no guarantee his success would continue. Although she signed it, she claimed she was shocked when it was carried out quickly. She attacked the Council and banished Cecil. She claimed that the death warrant had been sent without her authority, but that was largely an attempt to placate France and Spain.

Spot the mistake

Below are a sample exam question and a paragraph written in answer to the question. What mistake is stopping the paragraph being of a high quality? Rewrite the paragraph so that it displays the qualities of at least Level 5. The mark scheme is on page 7.

'Elizabeth managed the presence in England of Mary Queen of Scots effectively.' How far do you agree?

> Elizabeth was concerned about the potential threat the presence of Mary posed to her security. Elizabeth could have brought Mary to court, but that would have simply led to her becoming the centre of factional plots against Elizabeth. Elizabeth could have returned Mary to Scotland, but she would have been blamed if Mary had been killed. Elizabeth kept Mary in jail, but was unable to prevent the outbreak of the Rebellion of the Northern Earls, soon after Mary's arrival in England in 1568. Elizabeth moved her south following the rebellion so that she was further away from centres of Catholic support, but she would always offer a potential focus for Catholics until she was finally executed in 1587.

Introducing an argument

Below are a sample exam question, a list of key points to be made in the essay, and a simple introduction and conclusion for the essay. Read the question, the key points and the introduction and conclusion. Rewrite the introduction and conclusion in order to develop an argument.

How serious a problem for Elizabeth was Mary Queen of Scots?

Key points

1   Mary had a strong claim to the English throne.

2   Mary was seen by many Catholics to be the legitimate ruler.

3   At the start of the period Mary had French support for her claim.

4   Mary was an anointed queen.

5   Mary was the centre of plots against Elizabeth.

6   After 1568 Mary was present in England.

Introduction

> There were many ways in which Mary Queen of Scots was a threat to Elizabeth. Mary was seen by some Catholics to be the rightful monarch as they did not recognise Henry VIII's marriage to Anne Boleyn. Mary was also a Catholic and this made her a threat. She was also a threat because she had support from France. However, she was not a threat as few people in England were willing to support plots and rebellions against Elizabeth. She was also not a threat as Spain would not help her take the throne.

Conclusion

> Thus we may see that there were many ways and times that Mary was a threat to Elizabeth. Her claim to the throne made her a threat as did support from France. She was Catholic and this could win her support as well. However, there were also ways in which she was not a threat as she was unable to get support.

Exam focus

Below is a model answer in response to an exam-style question. Read the answer and the comments around it.

How successful were Elizabeth I and her ministers in managing parliament?

Although there was some disagreement between parliament and the monarch and her ministers, for most of the time the relationship was one of co-operation and even when there was conflict it rarely lasted for a long time. There were clashes over parliamentary privileges and issues such as monopolies, religion and the succession, but through her personality, use of prerogative powers and charm she was largely successful in her management of parliament, seen most clearly in the considerable sums of money granted in the 1590s. However, although the techniques used by Elizabeth and her ministers to control parliament were generally effective it must also be remembered that MPs had much to lose by creating instability and it can even be argued that any opposition was not difficult to manage because it was neither organised nor strong enough to present a serious challenge to the queen.

> The opening paragraph establishes the debate and offers a clear view about the question.

The number of powers available to Elizabeth in order to manage parliament ensured that she was mostly successful. She possessed the ultimate weapon in that through her prerogative she had the power to summon, prorogue, adjourn and dissolve parliament. Elizabeth was therefore able to call them when she wanted and this was done only rarely, usually when she needed money, as in the 1590s to finance war. As she was able to obtain considerable sums from them, even during a period of rapid inflation and increasing financial pressure, it was evident that she was successful in achieving her goal. However, it was not just her powers that meant she was successful, as she was also helped by the fact that most MPs did not want to stay in London for too long as it was expensive. As a result, some did not attend and many who did were more concerned about local issues than national and therefore were not difficult to manage. On many occasions, once taxes had been granted, Elizabeth saw little need to prolong the session and many MPs were more than happy to return home, suggesting that the meetings were not difficult to manage. This is made even clearer by the lack of MPs who spoke in debates and the numbers who actually bothered to vote, suggesting that most matters were not controversial and therefore there was little difficulty in managing an institution that was largely subservient.

> The argument in the paragraph is balanced, with the first half outlining her powers that made it a success, but the second examining the attitudes of members.

> A judgement is reached about the issue.

The queen was very successful in preventing measures that she did not like as she had the power to veto bills. This power was used successfully in 1571 when she refused to introduce heavy fines for those who did not take communion in the Church of England as she feared that it would create recusants who did not attend. She also vetoed attempts to reform the Church in 1584–85, refusing to change the settlement that had been established at the start of her reign. Similarly, in 1572 she also blocked attempts to pass a bill declaring Mary Stuart could never be queen. However, she did not simply use the veto, but also managed parliament through concessions as was evident in the 1590s over monopolies or in 1566 when she allowed discussion about the succession 'out of pity', but only for that session, a condition that was made clear in her closing speech.

> The opening sentence introduces an idea which is developed in the paragraph with clear examples to support the claim.

As parliament was, until the 1590s, largely under the control of Elizabeth's councillors this usually made the task of management much easier. Councillors ensured that parliamentary business was under their control, drew up agendas and managed debates so that the royal will was usually achieved. They were also able to ensure that the Commons had less freedom of speech and cut down the time allowed for speeches. However, there were occasions when, due to the influence of her councillors, she was less successful in managing parliament, as the

> A further factor for the success is outlined.

events of 1571 revealed. Having failed to persuade Elizabeth at Council meetings to exclude Mary after the Ridolfi plot, Knollys and Croft, both councillors and supported by Bacon and Cecil, used parliament to put pressure on the queen to exclude Mary from the succession. Elizabeth was able to prevent this through her veto, but was forced to execute Norfolk. Similarly, in 1587 it was councillors who supported Cope's 'Bill and Book' and the queen had to intervene to stop it from proceeding, suggesting that when councillors supported MPs she had a far harder task managing parliament. Yet on other occasions Cecil guided legislation through the Commons and when he moved to the Lords he continued to give instructions and apply pressure, telling the Commons to put aside private bills and focus on commonwealth matters. As a result, for much of the time parliament was under the control of the queen and her ministers. However, when parliament was less successfully managed it was because Elizabeth's own ministers, who had been frustrated at their inability to achieve their aims through discussions in the Privy Council, used parliament to generate support for their cause in the hope of persuading Elizabeth to change her mind.

> Precise examples are used to support the argument over the importance of councillors and their support.

> The argument is balanced.

> A judgement is reached.

However, parliament itself was also supportive of the monarch. It was parliament who sent Peter Wentworth to the Tower in 1576 for offensive remarks against the queen. Despite this, there were times when it was much harder for Elizabeth to control parliament. In 1571 her suspension of Strickland for making radical proposals for Prayer Book reform caused such a storm that she never suspended an MP again for something said in the House. Although there were disagreements over issues of freedom of speech Elizabeth was able to maintain her prerogative intact, but parliament was much harder to manage in the 1590s and Elizabeth was forced to compromise over monopolies. Government was gradually losing control, in part because councillors who had been in the Commons were either dead or were too old. Parliamentary committees were also starting to seize the initiative and put forward policies instead of simply examine legislation, while the financial problems facing the government through war meant that the commons had a greater voice, forcing the government to pay greater attention to their complaints.

> A further factor is introduced.

> A balanced argument is pursued.

For much of Elizabeth's reign the management of parliament was not a difficult task. Much of the legislation concerned local issues that were not controversial, while Elizabeth and her ministers were able to control and manage debates. Any difficulties were the exception not the rule. However, there was a change in the 1590s and it was much harder for Elizabeth to manage parliament as the concessions over monopolies show. Despite this she preserved her powers intact, suggesting she was successful and with her Golden Speech of 1601 was still able to show how effectively she could use her charm to manage them.

> A balanced judgement is reached, which is a nuanced view of the first paragraph.

This is a well-focused answer, which considers a good range of issues in order to reach a judgement about the extent to which Elizabeth and her ministers were successful in managing parliament. There are some sections where the answer appears to become a little more descriptive, but in general the material is being used to support a line of argument. The quality of analysis and overall judgement would take the answer into the higher levels.

Planning an essay

The best essays are based on careful plans. Read the essay and the comments and try to work out the general points of the plan used to write the essay. Once you have done this, note down the specific examples used to support each general point and, where examples are either weak or lacking, use this book to help you find precise examples.

6 Elizabeth's management of financial, economic and social affairs

The financial and economic situation in 1558

Elizabeth had two types of income. Her ordinary income consisted of revenue from crown lands, customs duties, profits from justice and sources arising from patronage. She could also raise money from parliamentary taxation, known as extraordinary income, but this was supposed to be in times of emergency and was therefore not a regular source of income. This meant that she needed to ensure her policies were financed from her ordinary income. She also did not want to summon parliament too often as it gave MPs the opportunity to question her decisions. High levels of taxation could also lead to resistance and unrest.

Debts from Mary I

Elizabeth inherited a debt of £227,000. This had been largely caused by the war with France. Much of the debt was owed to the Antwerp Exchange, which was the money market for Northern Europe where merchants and financiers gathered because trade routes met there, and Elizabeth had to pay 14 per cent interest on the loan.

Marian financial reforms

Mary had introduced some reforms to make financial administration more efficient; most notably the Book of Rates for customs duties had been revised (see page 76). Mary also collected about three-quarters of crown revenue into the **Exchequer**, which meant it had a better idea of the financial situation and it also prevented duplication of officials. Elizabeth also inherited the services of William Paulet, Marquis of Winchester, who was highly experienced as Lord Treasurer.

The role of Sir Thomas Gresham

She also had the advice of the financier, Sir Thomas Gresham. He identified three problems that Elizabeth faced:
- **debasement** of the coinage, which had started under Henry VIII
- the cost of war and the loans that were needed to fund it
- the privileges of the **Hanseatic League** as they carried the wool from England.

He argued that Elizabeth needed to maintain an excellent credit rating so loans could be raised easily. He tried to persuade **William Cecil** to relax the laws on usury so that some interest and more money could be raised in England. In 1571 Cecil finally agreed and 10 per cent interest could be charged on loans.

Elizabeth and her debts

Not only was Elizabeth prudent, but as a single woman the expenses of court were less than if she had a family. She did not embark on major building projects. By spending summers on 'progress' around her realm, staying with courtiers and ministers, she reduced the costs at their expense. Courtiers were expected to give her generous gifts, which boosted income. Most importantly, she avoided war as far as possible, and the financial problems she faced in the latter years of her reign were largely due to that issue.

She was so successful that by 1576 Sir Walter Mildmay, Chancellor of the Exchequer, was able to inform the House of Commons that she had removed the Marian debt and by 1584 she had a surplus of £300,000. This suggest that it was the wars against Spain and in Ireland that created the financial problems of the last years of her reign.

Spectrum of significance

Below are a key question on Elizabeth's financial problems and a list of possible points. Use your own knowledge and the information on the opposite page to reach a judgement about the relative importance of these points. Write the numbers on the spectrum below to indicate their relative importance. Having done this, write a brief justification of your placement, explaining why some of the factors are more important than others. The resulting diagram could be the basis of an essay plan.

How serious were the financial problems facing Elizabeth I in 1558?

1 Elizabeth inherited a debt of £227,000.

2 The rate of interest on the debt was 14 per cent.

3 Mary had reformed the Book of Rates for custom duties.

4 Elizabeth's expenses were less than if she had been married.

5 She was able to make peace with France and avoid war.

6 By 1576 she had removed the debt.

Least important ⟵ ⟶ Most important

Develop the detail

a

Below are a sample exam question and paragraph written in answer to this question. The paragraph contains a limited amount of detail. Annotate the paragraph to add additional detail to the answer.

'The Marian reforms were the most important reason Elizabeth was able to solve her financial problems.' How far do you agree?

Mary's financial reforms certainly helped Elizabeth reduce the debt she inherited from her half-sister. The reduction of the debt was important because of the rate of interest that was payable on it and the financial reforms from Mary's reign would ensure that Elizabeth's system was more efficient. As Elizabeth relied heavily on ordinary income the increase in customs brought about by Mary's reform was particularly important. The Marian reforms also improved financial efficiency as this meant that less money was wasted. Elizabeth was also fortunate that she inherited Mary's experienced Lord Treasurer and had the advice of an expert financier. However, it was not just the reforms of Mary's reign that enabled Elizabeth to solve her financial problems but also Elizabeth's prudence and careful management of money through a variety of schemes she pursued.

Sources of crown income and finance

The most important sources of income were crown lands, customs duties and parliamentary taxation, although there were other sources, such as the Church, and Elizabeth was also able to make efficiency savings.

Crown lands

Elizabeth was able to increase her revenue from crown lands from £86,000 to £111,000, but this was less of a gain than most nobles made during the same period. Elizabeth did not use short-term leases to increase rents and much crown land was on long-term leases. Elizabeth was reluctant to exploit her tenants.

Customs duties

Mary had revised the Book of Rates, which governed the collection of customs duties. The new rates came into force in 1558. More imports were subject to tax and the amount was increased substantially, sometimes by 100 per cent. As a result, revenue from customs rose:

- 1556–57   £29,315
- 1558–59   £82,797

However, this was not maintained and in the 1590s customs were bringing in £91,000, a figure which had scarcely kept pace with inflation. The only way to increase income from customs was by increasing trade or putting up the rates. She could not raise the rates as they had only just been revised.

Most of the value of exports was from woollen cloth, which made up 81 per cent of the exports, and this required new markets to be found if the amount was to increase. Elizabeth attempted to encourage the 'finishing' of cloth – the dyeing and dressing – to take place in England, as that was where the greatest value was added to cloth, but this had little success. Most clothiers still exported unfinished cloth.

The increase in rates also encouraged smuggling and measures to prevent it were difficult to enforce as there were not enough officials.

Parliamentary taxation

Elizabeth could ask parliament for money. There were two forms of taxation, the fifteenths and tenths, which raised about £30,000, and the subsidy, which brought in £100,000. Parliament usually granted one subsidy and two fifteenths and tenths, bringing in about £130,000. This was less than in the reign of Henry VIII. Assessments were made by the local gentry and wealthy landowners were usually underassessed. However, Elizabeth was reluctant to change the situation and employ professional collectors or demand they increase the assessments. With rising inflation, it further decreased the real value of taxation and Elizabeth was therefore failing to fully exploit this source of income.

Efficiency savings

Mary had reformed the financial situation (see page 74) and this increased efficiency. Paulet ended the practice of officials storing money in their own homes, often using it to speculate on their own behalf. However, as he got old this practice returned and, in 1571, £44,000 had been borrowed from royal funds by officials. Cecil and Mildmay introduced reforms to prevent it happening, but their success was limited.

Officials were not well paid and the situation was made worse by inflation, which only encouraged corruption.

A type of finance committee was established to draw up a budget and look at areas where cuts could be made, collect debts more effectively and consider the sale of crown lands.

Other income

The queen did gain income from the Church in the form of First Fruits and Tenths and grants in parliament. She also kept bishoprics vacant to gain their income. Money was collected from non-attendance at church and after 1581 recusancy fines were increased. None of these sources could be significantly increased.

Support or challenge?

Below is a sample essay question which asks you for a judgement on a statement. Using your knowledge and the information on the opposite page, decide whether these statements support or challenge the statement and tick the appropriate box.

'Elizabeth I was able to exploit her income in order to meet her financial needs.' How far do you agree?

	Support	Challenge
Revenue from crown lands increased considerably		
Long-term leases prevented Elizabeth from increasing rents		
Revenues from customs did not keep pace with inflation in the 1590s		
Elizabeth was unable to put up customs duties as they had been increased under Mary I		
Parliamentary subsidies were less than under the reign of Henry VIII		
The financial reforms of Mary Tudor had increased efficiency		
Taxation assessments were outdated		
Elizabeth was able to increase her income from the Church		

Turning assertion into argument

Below are sample exam question and a series of assertions. Read the question and then add a justification to each of the assertions to turn each into an argument.

How successful was Elizabeth I's financial policy?

Elizabeth I's financial policy was successful only in the period until the mid 1580s

_____

_____

However, Elizabeth was unable to meet the financial demands of her latter years

_____

_____

This situation was made worse by her reluctance to reform the financial system

_____

_____

Financial problems: inflation, war, administration and monopolies

Elizabeth faced a number of financial problems, particularly in the second half of her reign, which resulted in increasing pressure on her finances and challenged the financial security she had established in 1576.

Inflation

Inflation was a problem across Europe, but it was made worse by debasement in England in the 1540s. Although inflation had declined by the start of Elizabeth's reign, it increased again from the 1560s, resulting in a rapid rise in food prices. Public opinion had initially blamed it on the greed of landowners, but by the 1570s many were blaming increased **bullion supplies**, though this is doubted by historians who question how much Spanish bullion came to England. Other reasons, such as the population rise and war, were probably more significant.

It was a serious problem because Elizabeth struggled to increase her income. She attempted to tackle the problem by **recoinage**, but it had limited success and the outbreak of war caused a crisis since the supplies she needed cost more. It also had an impact on wage-earners as real wages did not keep pace with inflation. The situation was made worse in the 1590s by a series of bad harvests, which made the cost of food even greater.

The impact of war

War and unrest in the Netherlands had an impact on English trade. First, it led to restrictions on privileges of merchants, which resulted in the English leaving Antwerp for Emden. English piracy in the Channel and later in the New World also affected trade and therefore revenue from customs. However, there were occasions, as in the period 1577–80, when attacks on Spanish ships brought in revenue; similarly in 1587 when Drake seized £140,000. However, the greatest impact was the cost of warfare. In 1585, through the Treaty of Nonsuch, Elizabeth pledged to provide the Dutch rebels with a force costing £126,000 per annum. The war in the Netherlands would cost £2 million, support for Henry of Navarre in France was over £500,000, the Armada campaign of 1588 £161,000 and the campaign to crush the Tyrone Rebellion in Ireland £2 million. This obviously put a great strain on resources as Elizabeth's ordinary sources of revenue brought in only £300,000 by 1600. Warfare forced Elizabeth to use her savings and then resort to extraordinary methods of finance.

Monopolies

The granting of exclusive rights to particular trades or manufacturers was one way Elizabeth raised money in the period. These **monopolies** were used to reward courtiers, but they also prevented competition and led to a rise in prices. The parliaments of 1597 and 1601 attacked the practice, and in light of the social problems of the 1590s (see page 90) Elizabeth made concessions, suspending some grants and revoking those which were harmful. A proclamation soon followed ending monopolies on salt, vinegar and starch, which were everyday necessities. In 1587 parliament had also attacked purveyance, which was the crown's right to buy goods at less than market prices, and was a regular occurrence when supplying the army and navy. Elizabeth promised to reform, but any change would increase the cost for the government.

Administration

Elizabeth attempted to make efficiency savings (page 76) to help reduce costs. She also issued a new coinage, started in 1560, to try to end inflation but this did not succeed. Loans had to be raised in Antwerp, which led to a fall in the value of the pound. The government also attempted to reduce imports, but this led to trade embargoes.

With bad harvests in the 1580, Elizabeth introduced a **Book of Orders** in 1586, which instructed **Justices of the Peace (JPs)** that there was to be no hoarding of grain. Corn was to be available in small amounts so the poor could afford it. As conditions worsened in the 1590s, further legislation was introduced. JPs were to fix wage rates, manufacturing was further regulated and Acts were passed to help the poor (see page 82). As the period progressed the government was intervening more and more in the economy.

(!) Delete as applicable **a**

Below are a sample exam question and a paragraph written in answer to this question. Read the paragraph and decide which of the possible options (in bold) is most appropriate. Delete the least appropriate options and complete the paragraph by justifying your selection.

How serious were the financial problems Elizabeth faced in the period after 1588?

Elizabeth had been **very/mostly/somewhat/not very** successful in her financial measures in the period up to 1588. The situation **improved/remained the same/declined** as a result of inflation which had a **severe/limited** impact on the value of royal income. Elizabeth attempted to solve the problem by recoinage and this had a **significant/limited** impact which **improved/remained the same/declined** with the outbreak of war. The outbreak of war made the problem **worse/less severe** because of the impact it had on the cost of supplies and the situation **improved/remained the same/got worse** in the 1590s with a series of poor harvests. Income further **increased/remained the same/declined** as a result of the impact of war on the cloth trade. Although Drake and others were able to seize Spanish bullion and treasure ships, the cost of war in the Netherlands, against Spain and the unrest in Ireland meant that Elizabeth's financial problems **got worse/stayed the same/improved** during the 1590s.

_____

_____

_____

_____

(!) Complete the paragraph **a**

Below are a sample question and a paragraph written in answer to this question. The paragraph contains a point and examples, but lacks a concluding explanatory link back to the question. Complete the paragraph, adding this link in the space provided.

'It was only the demands of war that created financial problems for Elizabeth in the period after 1580.' How far do you agree?

Elizabeth I had been able to establish financial security by 1576. War put increased stress on the financial system as Elizabeth had to fund conflicts in the Netherlands, against Spain and suppress unrest in Ireland. Some of the costs were offset by the seizure of Spanish bullion by Drake and other privateers, but the cost of the war in the Netherlands was some £2 million, support for Henry of Navarre against Spain £500,000, the Armada £160,000 and the suppression of Tyrone's rebellion £2 million. Not only did these costs put a strain on resources, but they far exceeded Elizabeth's ordinary income of £300,000. Warfare forced Elizabeth to use up savings and rely on extraordinary sources of income. The value of this income was further hit by inflation, which peaked in the 1590s, at the very time Elizabeth's expenditure on warfare was hitting its peak.

_____

_____

_____

_____

Overseas trade

Overseas trade was an important source of income through customs duties. However, in terms of the export of English goods, most of it was unfinished cloth which went through Antwerp, where the merchant adventurers had their base. There were other developments, with the Muscovy Company developing the Russian market and some merchants developing contacts with Guinea. American trade was controlled by the Spanish and trade with the Near and Far East under the control of the Portuguese and Venetians.

Developing new markets

It was important to develop new markets for a number of reasons:
- Demand at home and in Europe for woollen products declined.
- Rebellion and unrest led to the decline in Antwerp.
- Trade embargoes followed English support for the Dutch rebels and war with Spain.

The Muscovy Company

The Company had been set up in 1555 during the reign of Mary. Investors bought shares in companies such as this and received a proportion of the profits in relation to their investments. Woollen goods were sold to Russia and furs, hides, tar, timber, hemp and wax were brought back. There was also the hope that trade would extend down the River Volga to Persia so that silks and spices could be purchased and undercut the Portuguese and Venetians.

Slave trade

This was initially begun through John Hawkins who, on a voyage to the Canary Islands, had heard of the need for slaves in the West Indies. Given financial backing by friends, he sailed with three ships to Guinea, where 300 slaves were obtained. These were easily sold and the ships returned to England with hides, ginger and sugar. The profits were large, particularly if he could capture, rather than buy the slaves. The trade developed and more invested in it.

The Mediterranean

In the 1570s direct trade began with the Mediterranean, with silks, spices, olive oil and currants being imported. This was formalised in the 1580s with the establishment of the Levant Company, which traded with the Turkish empire, and the Venetian Company, which sent goods to the eastern Mediterranean.

The Baltic

Trade with the Baltic was dominated by the Hanseatic League, but in 1579 the Eastland Company was formed with a depot in Poland. It exported cloth and imported naval supplies. Although it was slow to grow, it did help ports on the east coast.

The Spanish Empire

At first it might have been the aim to trade legitimately with South America, but the hostility of the Spanish meant these activities were more like piracy.

The North-West Passage and North America

Attempts were made by Martin Frobisher and John Davis to discover a North-West Passage through which merchants could develop a route to the east. There were also developments on the east coast of America, which would have longer-term implications.

India

Closer links with India developed through the work of John Newberry and Ralph Fitch. This led to the formation of the East India Company in 1600.

However, developments were limited by a number of factors:
- European trade was hit by the Dutch revolt.
- The Hanseatic League resented attempts to trade in the Baltic.
- Faction at the Russian court made trade difficult.
- Trade with Persia was limited as the ruler did not want to anger Turkey.
- Spain claimed a monopoly of the slave trade.
- Weather conditions limited expeditions over the North-West Passage.

Therefore, although rewards could be considerable, there was the risk of losing profits, ships and men.

Simple essay style

Below is a sample exam question. Use your own knowledge and information on the opposite page to produce a plan for this question. Choose four general points, and provide three pieces of specific information to support each general point. The introduction should list the points to be discussed in the essay. The conclusion should summarise the key points and reach a judgement.

'The developing slave trade was the most successful area of expansion in trade in the Elizabethan period.' How far do you agree?

Introducing an argument

Below are a sample exam question, a list of points to be made in the essay, and a simple introduction and conclusion for the essay. Read the question, the key points, and the introduction and conclusion. Rewrite the introduction and conclusion in order to develop an argument.

How successfully was English overseas trade developed during the reign of Elizabeth I?

Key points

- Replace Antwerp as the major outlet for wool and cloth products
- The development of trade with Russia
- The slave trade
- The establishment of the Levant Company
- Conflict with the Spanish empire
- The North-West Passage
- The impact of the Dutch revolt
- The power of the Hanseatic League

Introduction

There was evidence of success in the development of overseas trade into new markets, but there was also some evidence of failure. Some of the projects did result in English merchants gaining access to new markets which were needed if trade was to grow. However, there were some areas where expansion was less successful and was blocked by other powers or groups.

Conclusion

The expansion of overseas trade away from the reliance on Antwerp did have some success during Elizabeth's reign, with new markets opening in a range of areas. Merchants were now able to look beyond the cloth market at Antwerp to other areas both inside and outside Europe. However, there were also some problems in expanding trade, with opposition from some countries who wanted to maintain a monopoly and in some areas where the scale of trade was quite small and could not replace Antwerp.

Poverty and the Poor Law

Poverty and vagrancy was an increasing problem for Elizabethan governments, but they were less aware of what was causing the rise or the best way to deal with the problem. The growing population was probably a major reason as the population rose from an estimated 2.8 million in the 1540s to 4.1 million by 1601. Another cause was the way soldiers and sailors were discharged, often with little money and a long way from home. Contemporaries often blamed **enclosure** and the conversion of arable land to pasture, as it needed fewer labourers.

The response of towns and cities

Towns and cities were more effective in dealing with the problem. Norwich is probably the best example, with begging forbidden and the establishment of regular contributions from householders. Towns such as Ipswich, Exeter and Cambridge introduced taxes and in York a daily payment was made available for the old and infirm.

The regulation of employment and the Statute of Artificers

Unemployment was a concern and therefore attempts were made to regulate employment, with the most significant legislation, the Statute of Artificers, introduced in 1563. Its terms included:

- those under 30 and unmarried had to serve an employer who needed them
- everyone was to work the land unless a scholar, at sea or in a skilled occupation
- wage rates were to be settled locally and announced by the JP
- hours of work were enforced
- seven-year apprenticeships for all who practised crafts.

The Act did not stop people moving to look for work and the Act was difficult to enforce. Casual day labourers were also used and they were brought in as required.

Government legislation

In the period from 1563 to 1601 a series of measures was introduced to deal with the problem of poverty and vagrancy. The lack of unrest and the longevity of the 1601 Act suggests they had some success.

1563 Alms Act

The deserving poor were to be helped by a Poor Rate. People were required to contribute to the rate and those who refused were encouraged by the bishop to pay.

1572 Poor Relief Act

Contributions to the Poor Rate were now made compulsory, but begging was licensed where relief could not be provided. Those begging without a licence were whipped and burned through the ear (ear boring).

1576 Act for the Relief of the Poor

Licences to beg were given to those who had lost their possessions or those who were poor and had particular needs. Large towns had to provide materials to put the idle poor to work. Persistent beggars were sent to **Houses of Correction**, which were established in every county.

1598 Act for the Relief of the Poor

Begging was forbidden, but the Poor Rate was still levied, although a maximum amount was set. JPs appointed Overseers of the Poor to provide materials to employ the able-bodied, but also to relieve the aged and infirm.

1598 Act for the Punishment of Rogues, Vagabonds and Sturdy Beggars

Ear boring was ended, but 'sturdy beggars' were whipped and returned to their place of birth. 'Dangerous rogues' were banished or sent to the galleys.

1601 Act for the Relief of the Poor

The 1598 Poor Law was made permanent.

The government now replaced the Church in providing for the poor and a distinction was made between the 'deserving' and 'undeserving' poor. The former were treated with sympathy, but others more harshly.

Identify an argument

Below are a sample exam question and two sample conclusions. One of the conclusions achieves a high level because it contains an argument (an assertion justified with a reason – a statement that explains or justifies something). The other achieves a lower level because it contains only description (a detailed account) and assertion (a statement of fact or an opinion which is not supported by a reason). Identify which is which. The mark scheme on page 7 will help you.

How serious was the problem of poverty and vagrancy in Elizabethan England?

Sample 1

Poverty and vagrancy were serious problems for Elizabeth due to a number of reasons. Probably the most important was the rapid growth in population from 2.8 million to 4.1, which put increased pressure on food supplies and caused them to rise rapidly, particularly in the 1590s, meaning that many could no longer afford to purchase grain. The problem was added to by a series of bad harvests in the 1590s which forced prices up even further and added to the problems facing those less well-off. The situation was further complicated by outbreaks of the plague and other epidemics which often resulted in the death of the breadwinner, leaving families without a regular source of income and forcing them into begging or vagrancy. The problem was further complicated by war which saw a large number of soldiers and sailors discharged from service a long way from home, but without the means to support themselves and who were therefore also forced into begging.

Sample 2

Poverty and vagrancy rose during the reign of Elizabeth I. There were changes in agriculture during the period. Many farms went from arable to sheep farming because of the demand created by the growth in the cloth trade, but sheep farming did not require as many people. A number of villages were abandoned and Acts were passed to prevent the conversion of land from arable to pasture. Writers at the time often claimed that enclosure was major problem, but they also blamed greedy landowners. At the same time men who had been in either the army or navy were being discharged. The population also rose from about 2.8 million in the 1540s to 4.1 million by the end of the sixteenth century.

 Develop the detail

Below are a sample exam answer and a paragraph written in answer to this question. The paragraph contains limited amount of detail. Annotate the paragraph to add additional detail to the answer.

How effective were the Elizabethan poor laws in dealing with the problem of poverty and vagrancy?

The government passed a large number of Acts to deal with the problem of poverty and vagrancy. The lack of social unrest in the 1590s, when there was great social distress, suggests that the Acts were largely successful. In particular, the government was effective in dealing with 'deserving' poor who were helped by a number of measures. However, their response to the 'undeserving' poor was much harsher and did little to deal with the problem. Despite this, the government had taken on responsibility for providing for the poor. There were some effective measures in terms of providing work for the able-bodied. However, in many areas it was local towns who led the way with a variety of measures to provide for their poor, some of which were later incorporated into government legislation.

Exam focus

Below is a model answer in response to an exam-style question. Read the answer and the comments around it.

How successful were Elizabeth I's financial policies?

Elizabeth came to the throne when finances were under strain, with a debt of £227,000, and yet by 1576 Sir Walter Mildmay, her Chancellor, was able to tell the House of Commons that she had 'delivered this kingdom from a great and weighty debt', suggesting that her policies in the first part of her reign were successful. It can also be argued that she was largely successful in the last part of the reign as by 1584 she had a surplus of £300,000 and when she died in 1603 she left a debt of £300,000, most of which would be met by the subsidy still to be collected and this despite a period of constant warfare and high levels of inflation.

> A very clear view is offered and a strong argument is put forward, with some convincing support.

However, it was not always Elizabeth's policies that resulted in the financial progress that was made. In part, her success was due initially to policies she inherited from her half-sister, Mary. The new Book of Rates increased revenue from customs and saw income rise from £29,000 in 1556–57 to £83,000 by 1559. At the same time, she also inherited Mary's financial advisors, such as William Paulet, a very experienced Lord Treasurer and had the advice of the financier Thomas Gresham, who was able to offer advice on the money markets, from which the monarchy had been forced to borrow. Therefore, initial success was due more to other factors rather than Elizabeth's policies.

> A balance to the opening paragraph is offered and the success is placed in context with the suggestion it was due less to Elizabeth's policies than those of Mary.

Despite the apparent success in eradicating debt, it was difficult for Elizabeth to exploit her sources of income and there were areas where Elizabeth was less successful. She was able to increase her revenue from crown lands only slightly from £86,000 to £111,000, which was less than many of her nobility. Not only was the queen unable to pursue the more aggressive land management systems the nobles pursued, but much crown land was rented out on long leases and therefore rents could not be increased in the short term to meet inflationary pressures. Elizabeth's government also brought in a new coinage in 1560, believing that this would help to reduce inflation. However, this was not successful, as many did not believe the new coins were accurately valued and prices did not go down. Similarly, although she was able to obtain money from the parliaments she summoned, she was both unwilling and felt unable to ask for it until it was absolutely essential in the late 1580s and 1590s for fear of angering MPs who could then insist on the redress of their grievances before granting supply. She was also unwilling to change the system whereby the local gentry assessed themselves and were seriously underassessed. She feared that a change in policy would alienate them and was unwilling to risk this as she relied on them for much of her administration. As a result, parliamentary taxation was not fully exploited, as both she and Cecil wanted to avoid the social disruption that they feared would follow a rise in taxation.

> Further balance to the opening is offered.

> Three policies are examined to show that not all were successful.

However, Elizabeth was more successful in dealing with debts through efficiency savings. She successfully avoided any lavish building projects which would have consumed large sums of money and was also able to avoid spending large sums by going on 'progress' during the summer months so that courtiers and ministers had to pay the costs of her entertainment. She also continued Mary's policy of collecting most revenue into the Exchequer, which was more efficient and meant that there was less duplication of officials. A small group of councillors also formed a virtual finance committee and drew up a budget so that savings could be made and debts collected. The employment of some 80 people in the Exchequer helped to ensure that the department was more efficient and saved money. However, Elizabeth was less successful in dealing with the salaries of officials. It might be argued that she was successful in preventing their salaries from rising, but this simply caused them to take income from unofficial sources, most notably payments for privileges which served only to weaken royal control.

Elizabeth was also successful in the early years of her reign in avoiding the high costs that warfare caused. By making peace with France at the start of her reign she reduced expenditure and this played a significant part in cutting the Marian debt and turning it into a surplus. This policy continued until 1585 when she was virtually forced into war against Spain, but by delaying it for so long or using other means, such as privateering to attack the Spanish, this policy of avoiding war was successful in keeping down expenditure. Moreover, when war did break out Elizabeth was successful in financing the war and was able to raise the large sums needed. The success of her financial policies in the 1590s was even more remarkable given the scale of inflation. It is true that much of the financing was by hand-to-mouth measures and there were occasions, as in 1588, when she was forced to borrow £56,000 from the City of London at 10 per cent interest. Given the cost, with over £2 million spent in Ireland, it was not surprising that, despite sizeable parliamentary subsidies, the cost could not be met. However, Elizabeth was able to meet much of it by selling crown lands. Therefore, although the surplus of £300,000 was spent, given that the cost of the war with Spain, unrest in Ireland and supporting the Dutch was some £4.5 million, it was remarkable that she kept the debt to manageable levels by her death.

In the short term Elizabeth's policies were successful as she was able to leave the crown little more in debt than when she inherited the throne, despite the cost of warfare in the last decade. However, in the long term it could be argued her policies were less successful as she was unable to secure a realistic assessment for parliamentary subsidies and survived by selling off large tracts of crown land. She also benefited greatly from the policies of Mary, but compared with other European monarchs, such as Philip II of Spain, her debts were small and England did not have to declare bankruptcy.

The paragraph analyses a range of financial policies and measures that were successful.

Although not a financial policy, it is relevant to the argument.

A convincing argument that she was successful because she was, at least in the short term, able to meet the needs of war.

A very strong conclusion, which offers a nuanced view comparing short- and long-term success as well as placing her performance in a wider European context.

This is a well-argued and balanced response, which is able to place Elizabeth's financial policies in their broader context in order to produce a high-level answer. Knowledge is used to support a clear and well-thought-through argument. There is a clear and supported judgement, which would ensure the answer reaches the higher levels.

Reaching the highest level

Using the comments and the mark scheme on page 7, make a list of additional features, both in terms of supporting detail, but also arguments, that would ensure that this response reaches the highest level. Remember that even an answer that is awarded full marks is not a perfect answer, but one that is best fit with the level descriptors in the mark scheme.

7 Elizabethan later years, 1588–1603

Defence of the royal prerogative and relations with parliament

Elizabeth might have hoped that her clear definition of what she regarded as the **royal prerogative** would have ended any attempts to undermine it. However, in the period after 1588 there was a new generation of MPs who were unhappy about some of her privileges. Although most had accepted her control over religion, there were a number who were less willing to accept her use of purveyance and **monopolies**.

Purveyance

In 1593 the Commons asked for a remedy over the issue of purveyance, but **William Cecil** replied that the request infringed royal prerogative and could not be debated. However, the queen accepted there was a problem and agreed to deal with it.

The succession

The MP Peter Wentworth had written a pamphlet in which he urged the queen to decide which claimant to the throne had the best claim. He had been imprisoned by the Council, but upon release discussed the matter with MPs outside parliament. This was breaking the law which did not allow parliamentary business to be discussed outside parliament. The Council sent him to the Tower, where he died in 1597. This ended the issue and preserved the queen's prerogative without her having to act.

Monopolies

The issue came to a head in 1597. Elizabeth had used monopolies to reward courtiers as the pressure of war meant little money was available for pensions. When the matter was raised, Elizabeth agreed that those monopolies which were responsible for rising prices on basic goods should be cancelled. However, the issue did not go away as she revoked only a few and issued new ones. Little action had been taken by the time parliament met in 1601. MPs were in general agreement that monopolies were being abused. The heated debates forced the queen to act. Although most MPs protested loyalty to Elizabeth, some blamed the queen. She told the Speaker she would act immediately and the worst were ended immediately while others were referred to the courts, which helped preserve the royal prerogative. The queen also used her considerable skill in giving some MPs an audience and then making her famous Golden Speech.

Relations with parliament

Because of the war with Spain, Elizabeth summoned four parliaments in the period after 1588 as she needed money. The continued demands brought on by the war did mean that later parliaments were less willing to grant supply, but this must also be seen in the context of the poor economic situation.

However, in 1589 they granted twice the usual amount, but this worried some who thought it might create a precedent. It was therefore agreed that this would not be the norm and that it would be collected over a longer period so people did not pay any more. Throughout the period, even if parliament had to be persuaded, money was raised because of the foreign situation (see page 88). However, the demand for money did mean that the government had to listen to parliament's concerns and complaints. The monopolies debate is evidence that the queen had to use her charm and skills to diffuse the situation. It might be argued that the government was gradually losing control in the Commons as many councillors who had managed business for the queen were now either dead or were sitting in the Lords. Parliamentary committees were also starting to seize the initiative and put forward new policies, rather than just examine legislation.

Despite these developments, Elizabeth's relationship with parliament was usually harmonious and clashes usually had little long-term significance as the opposition was neither organised nor strong enough.

Turning an assertion into argument a

Below are a sample exam question and a series of assertions. Read the question and then add a justification to each of the assertions to turn it into an argument.

How successfully did Elizabeth defend the royal prerogative in the period after 1588?

MPs were able to successfully challenge some of Elizabeth's prerogative powers

_____

_____

However, Elizabeth's skill and charm limited the impact

_____

_____

The Council also helped preserve the queen's prerogative

_____

_____

Develop the detail a

Below are a sample exam question and a paragraph written in answer to the question. The paragraph contains a limited amount of detail. Annotate the paragraph to add additional detail to the answer.

'Elizabeth's relationship with parliament was poor in the period after 1588.' How far do you agree?

The demands of war meant that Elizabeth summoned parliament more frequently in the latter years of her reign. This gave parliament the opportunity to raise issues and demand that their grievances were addressed before money was granted. However, at times they did supply considerable sums, although such grants were made with qualifications. The debates over monopolies also revealed problems in the relationship and Elizabeth was forced into making some concessions, but these were not always put into practice, making the situation worse and causing further complaints. However, Elizabeth was able to use her charm and political skill to keep support. Her management of the Commons was not helped by a number of developments. However, despite these developments the clashes had little long-term impact.

The impact of the war with Spain

War dominated the last years of the reign. Elizabeth had been able to delay the conflict as she feared the financial problems it would create and the possibility of defeat at the hands of the major European power. The war drained England both in terms of men and money. However, by the time of Elizabeth's death war-weariness had set in and many were glad that peace was made with Spain in 1604 and that unrest in Ireland had been crushed.

The 1588 Armada

The defeat of the Armada played a significant role in the growing pride people were starting to feel in the country. It also did much for Elizabeth's image and the belief that divine providence had intervened on the side of the English, which was a strong weapon in the propaganda war against Spain. However, it had forced the queen to obtain forced loans of £75,000 from wealthy subjects and borrow £56,000 from the City of London at 10 per cent interest.

Later Armadas and war in France and the Netherlands

Elizabeth was not convinced that victory in 1588 had completely wiped out the Spanish navy and invasion scares were present throughout the 1590s. The continued fighting, both at sea and on land, supporting Henry of Navarre and the Dutch rebels, consumed large amounts of money, giving Henry £20,000 in 1589, although she did expect it to be returned, and also sending 10,000 troops in 1590–91.

The impact on finances

The costs of war continued to grow, with nearly 100,000 men sent to fight in the period, all of which had to be paid for, and the total expenditure was some £4.5 million, with £2 million of that spent in Ireland. Only half was met from parliamentary grants and the surplus that had been built up was spent. In 1599–1600 Elizabeth was forced to sell crown lands and also considered selling some jewellery because the situation was so bad. She reduced expenditure at court, particularly on patronage, and kept positions vacant to avoid paying salaries. The lack of patronage encouraged bribery and corruption, and played a role in the issuing of monopolies (see page 86).

The impact on politics

The continuation of the war did cause debate among councillors. Although they all agreed that the war should be prosecuted, there was some disagreement as to how. Cecil preferred to respond to situations, but younger councillors argued for a more proactive policy with naval attacks against Spain. Divisions over the nature of the war resulted in every decision being affected and factions developing. **Essex** had become a national hero because of his attack on Cadiz in 1596 and he pushed for a more active policy, but Cecil wanted to bring about peace, particularly after Henry IV of France made peace with Spain, but Essex opposed it. The factional fighting would continue even after Cecil's death in 1598 as his role was taken up his son **Robert Cecil**. The situation was not helped by Elizabeth's failure to have a clear policy. Although she was aware of the dangers of a more 'forward policy', she sometimes gave in to pressures from courtiers and this served only to show a lack of coherence in policy.

Support or challenge a

Below is a sample exam question which asks how far you agree with a specific statement. Below this is a series of general statements which are relevant to the question. Use your own knowledge and the information on the opposite page to decide whether the sources support or challenge the statement in the question and tick the appropriate box.

'The most important impact of the war with Spain was financial.' How far do you agree?

	Support	Challenge
The war with Spain created a sense of pride and nationalism		
The war helped reinforce Elizabeth's image		
The war forced Elizabeth to obtain loans from the city and wealthy people		
Despite victory over the Armada in 1588 there were still invasion scares in the 1590s		
Elizabeth was forced to spend the surplus that had been accumulated		
Crown lands were sold and expenditure at court was reduced to help meet costs		
The war led to divisions among councillors as to how it should be prosecuted		
There were divisions between Cecil and Essex over the war		

Delete as appropriate a

Below are a sample exam question and a paragraph written in answer to the question. Read the paragraph and decide which of the possible options (in bold) is most appropriate. Delete the least appropriate options and complete the paragraph by justifying your selection.

How serious an impact did war have on the Elizabethan regime after 1588?

The impact of war on the Elizabethan regime was **limited/great/severe.** The defeat of the Armada in 1588 was used as propaganda and **brought an end/failed to end** the Spanish threat. The continued fighting was a **considerable drain/moderate drain/had little impact** on royal finances which were **easily able/struggling/failed** to meet the demands. The costliest of the enterprises was **the war in the Netherlands/France/Ireland/against Spain,** with some £2 million spent and parliamentary grants were **more than adequate/covered/did not meet** this cost. However, it was not just finances that were impacted by the war. The war **united/divided** the Council and resulted in an **increase/decrease** in factional conflict between Cecil and Essex, particularly after the latter's success at Cadiz. The situation was made **more difficult/less difficult** because overall policy **was coherent/lacked coherence.**

Social and economic problems

The latter years of Elizabeth's reign were plagued by rising inflation (see pages 78) and, partly as a result, an increase in both poverty and vagrancy (see page 82). However, the situation was made worse by a series of bad harvests and, therefore, food shortages, which created some unrest.

Harvests

There were some bad harvests in the 1580s, which had already resulted in an increase in the price of bread, but a run of bad harvests from 1594 to 1598 made the situation even worse. By 1596 the average price of wheat had doubled compared with normal times as bad weather had a serious impact. Those who suffered the most were those living close to subsistence level as the cheaper grains, oats and rye, rose as much or even more than wheat. The situation was made more difficult because poor transportation meant it was harder to move supplies from areas where there was a surplus. There were even deaths reported from malnutrition. In 1595–97 the death rate increased 50 per cent. The rise in prices also increased poverty and the government passed a series of laws to deal with the problem (see page 82), but also introduced measures to keep land under cultivation and to prevent depopulation and the destruction of farms.

Plague

As people were debilitated by a lack of food, they had less resistance to the plague. Parish registers show that nearly every town was affected in 1596 and 1597. Books of Orders attempted to introduce quarantine measures, but these were often defied. The death of the breadwinner could have a devastating impact and add to the problem of poverty.

Unrest

Given the difficulties, the government was fearful of unrest. There was much grumbling and some refused to pay ship money, while others complained about purveyance and monopolies, and some complained about the raising of troops. Apprentices caused trouble in London, such that the goose fair was cancelled in 1593, and in 1595 some youths were hanged for causing trouble on Tower Hill.

Food riots

There were food riots in Kent in 1595, Sussex, Somerset and Norfolk in the period from 1596 to 1598. There had also been unrest in Ipswich in 1586.

Oxfordshire, 1596

The government was paranoid about unrest, perhaps because it lacked a police force, and this was seen clearly in its reaction to events in Oxfordshire in 1596. The protest in north Oxfordshire was supposedly due to enclosure. There had been a previous protest when 60 men had asked the Lord Lieutenant for help for the poor and starving. The protestors were to meet on Enslow Hill, which had been the site of protest in 1549, then throw down enclosures, seize guns and march on London to join with the apprentices. However, the plot was betrayed to the government, who either saw it as a serious threat or just wanted to make an example of the protestors. The five ringleaders were arrested, taken to London and charged with treason. Some 25 others were questioned locally.

However, the rising was hardly a serious threat. It attracted only a small number despite the conditions and many who had been urged to join had refused. Only four actually turned up at Enslow Hill. Despite the harsh government response they also passed some legislation to tackle the problems the unrest had raised. In 1597 the Tillage Act was passed to reverse **enclosure** that had been carried out since 1588. The lack of trouble is an indication that government measures were successful in controlling the disquiet and that many no longer saw rebellion as the way to bring about changes.

! Complete the paragraph a

Below are a sample exam question and a paragraph written in answer to this question. The paragraph contains a point and specific examples, but lacks a concluding explanatory link back to the question. Complete the paragraph, adding this link in the space provided.

How serious a threat to Elizabeth were the social and economic problems in the 1590s?

The last decade of Elizabeth's reign witnessed a large number of social and economic problems. The problem of inflation resulted in an increase in poverty and vagrancy and this was made worse by a series of bad harvests from 1594 to 1598. The bad harvests created some unrest as the price of grain doubled. However, the government responded with a series of measures, most notably a number of poor laws which helped to control the situation. There was also unrest in Oxfordshire due to high levels of taxation and enclosure. However, only a few turned up to the meeting place at Enslow Hill, but the government still took severe action, with the ringleaders charged with treason.

_____

_____

_____

_____

⬥ Eliminate irrelevance a

Below are a sample exam question and a paragraph written in answer to the question. Read the paragraph and identify parts of the paragraph that are not directly relevant to the question. Draw a line through the information that is irrelevant and justify your deletions in the margin.

Assess the reasons why there was so little unrest in the 1590s.

Government legislation, particularly the poor laws, played a crucial role in ensuring that there was little unrest. Futhermore, the government took action to try to secure food supplies by passing the Tillage Act, which reversed enclosure that had been carried out since 1588. It appeared as if many had realised that rebellion and riot was not the way to solve problems, with only five people turning up for the Oxfordshire rising in 1596, and that it was better to use parliament to deal with problems. However, there was unrest in parliament as MPs put pressure on the queen to repeal monopolies and raised objections about purveyance. This forced the queen to repeal some monopolies and use her skill through her Golden Speech to revive support for her rule. Despite the Oxfordshire rising and a few food riots in places such as Kent and Somerset, unrest was limited, suggesting that government measures were largely successful and that the only unrest was in parliament.

Ireland and Essex

The trouble Elizabeth faced in Ireland, the Tyrone Rebellion, was the most serious unrest of the period, while the Essex rising in 1601, although it had the potential to be a threat, was easily crushed.

Ireland

Rebellion in Ireland was led by the Earl of Tyrone and it lasted from 1598 to 1603. The situation was made more threatening as it was feared that discontented Irishmen would allow Spanish troops to land and use it as a base from which to attack England. It was also a challenge as it was the first national revolt in Ireland and attracted support from a wide area. Tyrone was able to defeat the English at Yellow Ford in 1598, seize Munster and take much of Ireland, with only Leinster holding out. Tyrone had the resources of Ulster to support his men and his forces were well trained and often led by captains who had served in Elizabeth's armies. He was also able to secure reinforcements from Scotland, while he was a skilled leader, an expert in ambush and knew the area.

The Earl of Essex was sent to deal with the problem, with the largest army sent to Ireland in the Tudor period of 16,000 men. The Council provided a large amount of resources, but Essex was unable to deal with the problem. When he marched north to face Tyrone he took only 4000 men and avoided battle. He then came home, disobeying orders. He was replaced by Lord Mountjoy, who was more effective. He conciliated many of the Irish, who disliked Tyrone's rule, captured some of the leaders and defeated a Spanish force that landed at Kinsale in 1602. He then advanced on Ulster, where, a few days after the queen's death, Tyrone surrendered.

The Essex rebellion, 1601

Essex was one of the younger generation of courtiers who rose to prominence in the later part of Elizabeth's reign. He first came to prominence after serving under Leicester in the Netherlands and won Elizabeth's favour when he came to court on return. However, he was headstrong, joining the expedition to Lisbon in 1589 against the queen's orders. His rivalry with Robert Cecil weakened his position and his failure to secure promotion for Francis Bacon in 1593 damaged his reputation as he seemed unable to fulfill his duty as a patron. Similarly, he failed to get offices for his supporters in 1597 when Lord Cobham died. However, he had won praise for his role in the expedition to Cadiz in 1596, but Cecil gained by his absence, becoming Principal Secretary.

Essex reacted badly when he did not get his own way. In 1598 he had angered the queen during discussions about who should be sent to Ireland and, although he was sent, the queen slapped him in the face when he turned his back on her. His role in Ireland (see above) further damaged his reputation. His return, without permission, resulted in him being placed under house arrest.

Essex had built up a party at court and had support in the City of London. However, his defiance of the queen's will on returning resulted in his power being further reduced. By sending Mountjoy to Ireland she took away one of his supporters and then removed his monopoly on sweet wines, which was his main source of income and left him under pressure from his creditors. This caused Essex to embark on treasonable actions. He made contact with James VI of Scotland, commissioned a performance of Shakespeare's *Richard II*, which included the deposition of a monarch by a noble to save the country from misrule. The next day he attempted to raise a rebellion in London and take control of Whitehall. He hoped to play on the unpopularity of Cecil, but many of his supporters did not act and he had overestimated public support. The rising was easily crushed and the leniency with which it was treated, with only six executions, suggests that the government saw the event as no more than a nuisance.

The removal of Essex did mean that the Cecil faction would dominate, with government dominated for the first time by one faction.

Spider diagram

Use the information on the opposite page and page 90 to add detail to the spider diagram on the causes of Essex's rebellion.

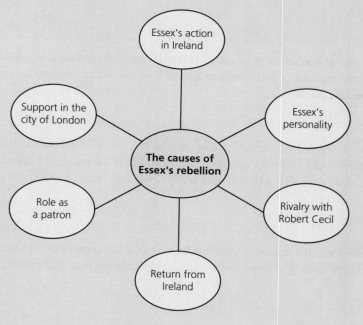

Essex's action in Ireland

Support in the city of London

Essex's personality

The causes of Essex's rebellion

Role as a patron

Rivalry with Robert Cecil

Return from Ireland

You're the examiner

a

Below are a sample exam question and a paragraph written in answer to the question. Read the paragraph and the mark scheme provided on page 7. Decide which level you would award the paragraph. Write the level below, along with a justification for your decision.

'Tyrone's rebellion was not a serious threat to Elizabeth.' How far do you agree?

Tyrone's rebellion was more of a nuisance than a threat to Elizabeth. Although it did provide Spain with the potential of a landing base from which to launch an attack against England, their forces when they did land at Kinsale were easily defeated. Instead it was the cost to Elizabeth, at a time of rising prices and warfare against Spain, that meant that Ireland was a drain on resources rather than a threat. Although English forces were defeated at Yellow Ford in 1598 and Essex failed to defeat Tyrone, the rebellion was not a direct threat to Elizabeth's power. Mountjoy was able to conciliate many of the Irish, who were already fed up with the nature of Tyrone's rule, and was easily able to advance on Ulster and force him to surrender, and with the same number of men as Essex it had been possible to restore order provided leadership was effective, further evidence that the unrest was not a serious threat but a nuisance.

Level:

Reason for choosing that level:

_____

_____

Elizabeth's reputation

The problems that Elizabeth faced after the defeat of the Armada have led some to question her popularity in the period from 1588 to 1603. There was some evidence that her position and image was undermined.

Scandals

A series of scandals undermined her authority at court. Raleigh was disgraced for making Bess Throckmorton pregnant and the Earl of Southampton had to leave the country when his affair with Elizabeth Vernon became public.

Criticism

The economic crisis of the 1590s did lead to an increase in criticism, with some commenting that 'we shall never have a merry world while the queen liveth'. Scandalous stories also emerged, with rumours the queen had had three children by different nobles or that Leicester had murdered the children.

Court

Attendance at court declined and the aristocracy were reluctant to accompany her on progress in 1600. Elizabeth also withdrew more and more from court and spent more time in her own apartments.

Appearance

As Elizabeth got older her looks diminished and it did not help her reputation. Some younger courtiers mocked her red wig. In 1596 the Council issued a proclamation stating that unseemly portraits would be destroyed, suggesting that some had been produced, which threatened her image. A formalised version of her face for use in paintings was produced by Nicholas Hilliard and was to be inserted into different pictures.

However, despite these difficulties, there is much evidence to suggest that she maintained her reputation, with plays and pageants still extolling her virtues and the Accession Day Tilts celebrating her accession on 17 November each year.

Progresses

Elizabeth still went on progress and took part in hunting and hawking. Ambassadors were still entertained and reported favourably on her. She was still dancing, even if less frequently. All of this helped to preserve to some extent the image of her youthfulness.

Parliament

Her final parliament witnessed considerable praise for her and her **Golden Speech** reduced some members to tears, suggesting that she had not lost her political touch or ability to win support through flattery.

This evidence suggests that she still maintained support. Her use of propaganda to reinforce her image certainly helped, particularly that of the Virgin Queen, who was a devoted ruler and abandoned her own happiness for the sake of the country. Increasingly, she was portrayed as Gloriana or the Virgin Queen, with virginity being used as a symbol of power. However, it might be argued that the representations of Gloriana were to disguise anxieties about her age, possible death and the succession.

Simple essay style

Below is a sample exam question. Use your knowledge and information on the opposite page to produce a plan for this question. Choose four general points and provide three pieces of specific information to support each general point. Once you have planned your essay, write the introduction and conclusion for the essay. The introduction should list the points to be discussed in the essay. The conclusion should summarise the key points and justify which point was the most important.

To what extent was Elizabeth's image undermined in the period from 1588 to 1603?

 Recommended reading

Below is a list of suggested further reading on this topic.

- *England 1485–1603*, pages 256–59, Mary Dicken and Nicholas Fellows (2015)
- *Elizabeth, The Forgotten Years*, John Guy (2016)
- *Tudor Britain*, pages 175–83, Roger Lockyer and Dan O'Sullivan (1998)
- *The Reign of Elizabeth*, pages 283–94, Barbara Mervyn (2001)
- *Elizabeth I and the Government of England*, Chapter 7, Keith Randell (1994)
- *The Reign of Elizabeth*, pages 115–25, William Simpson (2001)

Exam focus

Below is a model answer in response to an exam-style question. Read the answer and the comments around it.

'The most serious problem for Elizabeth I and her government in the years from 1588 to 1603 was the unrest in Ireland.' How far do you agree?

The years from 1588 to 1603, despite the victory over the Armada in 1588, are often seen as difficult years for the monarch, suggesting that the problems she faced were serious. There were certainly a number of problems for her, including the unrest in Ireland, but also at home, the continued war with Spain and its financial implications, while there were also clashes with parliament over issues such as purveyance and monopolies. However, the most serious problem for Elizabeth I and her government were the problems of inflation and poor harvests as they were out of her control and all the government could do was to try to lessen the impact on many of the population.

A range of issues or problems is raised and a clear view as to the most serious is offered.

The Tyrone Rebellion in Ireland from 1594 to 1603 was a problem for Elizabeth and her governments. It took the government a long time to crush and, at a time of other wars and unrest, as well as financial problems, was a drain on royal finances as it cost £2 million, but even that was less than the money spent on aiding the Dutch, suggesting that was more serious. However, it was serious in that English forces were defeated at Yellow Ford in 1598, while the resources that Tyrone had with Ulster, and his ability to raise a national rebellion, meant that it would be hard to crush. Despite this, it was less of a threat to Elizabeth and her government as the unrest was not in England and did not directly threaten the Tudor monarchy. Moreover, once Mountjoy replaced Essex as Lord Deputy he was quite quickly able to defeat the Spanish who had landed at Kinsale in 1602 and advance on, and defeat Ulster. This fairly quick victory once Essex was replaced further suggests that the rising was not such a threat and it was only prolonged because of Essex's mistakes.

The relative seriousness of Ireland is raised, but the point about the Dutch could be expanded.

There is a balanced discussion about the Irish issue and a supported judgement is reached.

In comparison the social and economic problems of inflation and food shortages that Elizabeth faced in the 1590s were more serious. Although they provoked little unrest, with the Oxfordshire Rising of 1596 attracting only five rebels, they were problems that the government was unable to solve. Inflation, due largely to a rise in population, was out of the government's control and was more serious than unrest in Ireland as it impacted on the government's ability to pay for an army in Ireland to crush the unrest as well as on food prices for ordinary people, which rose dramatically in the 1590s. The price of food was made even worse by a run of bad harvests from 1594 to 1598, with the average price doubling in 1596 compared with normal times. Government legislation attempted to ensure food was available, but it was unable to prevent deaths from malnutrition in Newcastle or the death rate rising by some 50 per cent in 1596–97. However, shortages also meant that people were less resistant to the plague and this added to the problems as many families lost their breadwinner and went into poverty, with the result that the number of vagabonds registered and punished after 1598 increased. The amount of government legislation, in terms of the Poor Law and attempts to limit enclosure through Acts to preserve land under cultivation and to prevent depopulation, let alone the severe action taken against the Oxfordshire protestors, shows how seriously they viewed the situation.

An explanation as to why it was serious is offered.

A direct comparison of the seriousness is made and explained.

A full explanation, with excellent detailed support as to why it was a serious problem, is given.